Programming Backend with Go

Build robust and scalable backends for your applications using the efficient and powerful tools of the Go ecosystem

Julian Braun

Published by: GitforGits

Publisher: Sonal Dhandre

www.gitforgits.com

support@gitforgits.com

Printed in India

First Printing: April 2024

ISBN: 9788119177998

Cover Design by: Kitten Publishing

Prologue

You have arrived at "Programming Backend with Go." Hi! I'm Julian Braun, and I can't wait to show you all the cool stuff about Go backend development. Working with Go for many years has shown me how effective and efficient it is for building scalable, high-performance backend systems. I hope that this book will be useful to you whether you are an experienced developer or just getting your feet dipped in the world of backend programming. The Google Go language, also known as Golang, is known for its simplicity, efficiency, and dependability. When speed and scalability are of the utmost importance, it excels in backend development. We will build real-world apps and services that can handle the demands of modern web environments by exploring how to harness Go's full potential throughout this book.

To get things rolling, we'll setup our development environment and make sure you have everything you need to get things done. I'll show you how to set up Visual Studio Code, install Go, and use Go modules to manage dependencies. A well-configured environment can greatly enhance your productivity and development ease, so this foundational step must be taken for anyone interested in diving into Go programming. After everything is ready to go, we will learn using Go's net/http package to build web servers. The book will teach you the ins and outs of serving static files, responding to requests, and routing various URLs to their respective handlers. As a foundation for more advanced topics, these skills are the bedrock of web development.

In subsequent sections, we will learn more complex routing methods implemented within the gorilla/mux package. With this robust library, you can easily build sophisticated web applications with more expressive and flexible URL handling. Additionally, we will discuss error handling, custom handlers, and middleware to make sure your applications are strong and easy to maintain.

Extensive coverage of security will be provided, as it is an essential component of backend development. You will discover how to construct secure apps that safeguard users' and data's information, from incorporating user authentication with OAuth2 and JWT to protecting your apps from typical vulnerabilities such as SQL injection and XSS attacks.

Go stands out due to its top-notch concurrency and parallelism support. We'll make the most of this by creating and implementing microservices. You will discover how to create, launch, and oversee scalable microservices using tools like Gin and Kubernetes. In addition, we will go over REST and gRPC for inter-service communication, which will equip you to construct service-oriented architectures that are both efficient and cohesive.

The ability to efficiently manage data is fundamental to many applications, and GORM will teach you just that. The fundamentals of CRUD operations as well as more complex features like transactions, migrations, and concurrency control will all be covered. In addition, you will gain knowledge of message brokering with Apache Kafka and NSQ, which will equip you to create apps that can manage asynchronous workloads with high throughput. We will learn tools like Delve, Testify, and GoMock, which are essential for any developer, to help with testing and debugging. You'll learn how to write thorough tests, mock dependencies, and debug applications to ensure reliability and bug-freeness.

At last, we'll talk about deployment strategies, such as blue-green, canary, and rolling. By learning how to automate your deployment process with AWS CodeDeploy, you can keep your applications running smoothly and up-to-date at all times. More than simply a book, "Programming Backend with Go" is an all-inclusive manual for turning you into an expert Go backend developer. The knowledge and abilities you acquire here will be very useful regardless of the complexity of the systems you're developing, be it simple web applications or complex distributed systems. Therefore, I say we jump right in and start making magic.

Content

Preface

Quickly introducing readers to Go and its ecosystem, the book walks them through installing the language and creating a development environment with Visual Studio Code. Next, it takes a baby step into learning the basics of building web servers with the net/http package, going over topics like routing, handling various HTTP methods, and the structures of requests and responses. Path variables, regex-based routing, custom handlers, and middleware are some of the advanced routing topics covered, which uses the robust gorilla/mux package. After introducing session and cookie management, the book moves on to user authentication, covering topics such as OAuth2 integration, JWT for secure APIs, and more.

The book then teaches various aspects of database integration with GORM, covering topics such as connecting to SQL databases, performing CRUD operations, managing migrations, and handling transactions and concurrency control. The Gin framework for designing and implementing microservices, REST and gRPC for inter-service communication, and Kubernetes for containerizing applications are also covered in detail. Also covered is message brokering with Apache Kafka and NSQ for asynchronous systems, which guarantees resilient systems and efficient message delivery. Secure coding practices, HTTPS with crypto/tls, avoiding SQL injections and XSS attacks, and configuration management with Viper are also one of the main goal of the book.

Last but not least, the book covers testing and debugging with tools such as Delve, Testify, and GoMock. It then teaches readers through various deployment strategies, such as blue-green, canary, and rolling deployments with AWS CodeDeploy. Utilizing Go's robust features and clean scripting capabilities, this book provides you with the necessary knowledge and skills to develop secure, scalable, and resilient backend systems.

This book takes its time to go over every important aspect of backend programming, from the fundamentals to more advanced techniques, so that you can become experts in Go scripting and all the things Go can do.

In this book you will learn how to:

- Get to know Go's ecosystem and tools to set up and configure backend development efficiently.
- Web servers can be easily built and managed using Go's net/http package for dynamic content delivery.
- Use gorilla/mux to implement advanced routing techniques for flexible URL handling.
- Implement strong API security with user authentication using OAuth2 and JWT.
- Make use of GORM's advanced capabilities of migrations and transactions, to integrate SQL databases.

- Use Gin, Kubernetes, and gRPC to build and launch scalable microservices.
- Make use of NSQ and Kafka for asynchronous processing.
- Prevent frequent vulnerabilities of SQL injection and XSS attacks.
- Use Testify, GoMock, and Delve to streamline testing and debugging.
- Use AWS CodeDeploy with blue-green and canary deployment strategies to deploy applications.

GitforGits

Prerequisites

Web developers, non-Go programmers, full-stack developers, and anyone else interested in learning the ins and outs of backend development with Go will find "Programming Backend with Go" to be an incredibly practical, use-case oriented, and illustrated learning resource.

Codes Usage

Are you in need of some helpful code examples to assist you in your programming and documentation? Look no further! Our book offers a wealth of supplemental material, including code examples and exercises.

Not only is this book here to aid you in getting your job done, but you have our permission to use the example code in your programs and documentation. However, please note that if you are reproducing a significant portion of the code, we do require you to contact us for permission.

But don't worry, using several chunks of code from this book in your program or answering a question by citing our book and quoting example code does not require permission. But if you do choose to give credit, an attribution typically includes the title, author, publisher, and ISBN. For example, "Programming Backend with Go by Julian Braun".

If you are unsure whether your intended use of the code examples falls under fair use or the permissions outlined above, please do not hesitate to reach out to us at support@gitforgits.com.

We are happy to assist and clarify any concerns.

Acknowledgement

I owe a tremendous debt of gratitude to GitforGits, for their unflagging enthusiasm and wise counsel throughout the entire process of writing this book. Their knowledge and careful editing helped make sure the piece was useful for people of all reading levels and comprehension skills. In addition, I'd like to thank everyone involved in the publishing process for their efforts in making this book a reality. Their efforts, from copyediting to advertising, made the project what it is today.

Finally, I'd like to express my gratitude to everyone who has shown me unconditional love and encouragement throughout my life. Their support was crucial to the completion of this book. I appreciate your help with this endeavour and your continued interest in my career.

Chapter 1: Understanding Go for Backend Development

Chapter Overview

This chapter is a good starting point for any prospective Go developer who wants to understand the ins and outs of backend programming. We will start with a high-level review of Go and its thriving ecosystem, then aim to get you acquainted with the language's capabilities and how they relate to current backend solutions. The next step is to install Go version 1.18 so that everyone is using the same version. Our next step will be to assist you in setting up Visual Studio Code, a powerful development environment. This editor is quite popular among Go developers, and it has several extensions that are expressly meant to make your life simpler.

This chapter will look at the mechanics of Go modules, a key feature added in recent Go versions that simplifies dependency management. This will enable us to better manage project dependencies and packages. Once your environment is ready, we will start by looking at the foundations of Go programming, such as grammar and structural patterns. This will equip you with a solid foundation in coding. In addition to these technical abilities, you will learn how to utilize Git for version control, which is essential for any modern software developer. This will help you to effectively manage and collaborate on code.

Along with the introduction, this chapter includes a sample application that will serve as a project throughout the book. Last but not least, learning Docker will teach you containerization, a critical skill for delivering consistent apps across several environments. After completing this chapter, you will have a basic understanding of Go backend development and be prepared to tackle more difficult subjects. You will also have all of the tools necessary to handle real-world programming challenges.

Go and its Ecosystem

Rob Pike, Ken Thompson, and Robert Griesemer designed Google's programming language Go. It's statically typed and compiled. It excels in backend development because it was developed to deal with the challenges of working with complex server-side systems. One of the key reasons why backend developers prefer Go is its simplicity, efficiency, and built-in support for concurrency.

Core Features

Go's syntax is clean and concise, which reduces the learning curve for new programmers and enhances code readability and maintainability. One of Go's distinguishing features is its approach to concurrency. Through Goroutines lightweight threads managed by the Go runtime, developers can easily implement scalable and high-performance backend systems. The language's performance is comparable to C or C++, thanks to its efficient compilation to machine code.

Standard Library

The Go standard library is robust and comes packed with functionality that can be leveraged to build complex backend systems. It includes powerful tools for handling HTTP requests, JSON encoding and decoding, and working with various types of databases. It also provides cryptographic libraries, logging libraries, and testing frameworks, which are essential for developing secure, reliable, and maintainable applications.

Go Modules and Package Management

Introduced in Go 1.11, modules are now the standard method for managing dependencies in Go applications. A module is a collection of Go packages stored in a file tree with a **`go.mod`** file at its root. The **`go.mod`** file defines the module's dependencies, and since Go 1.16, it automatically maintains and updates a graph of these dependencies. This makes it easier to manage the libraries your project relies on, ensuring consistent builds and simplifying code sharing across teams.

Popular Libraries for Backend Development

For routing and middleware, libraries such as **`gorilla/mux`** are invaluable. **`Gorilla/mux`** is an extensible request router and dispatcher that enables variable parts of the HTTP URLs to be captured and used as parameters, and it integrates seamlessly with the standard **`net/http`** library provided by Go.

When dealing with data, the **`gorm`** library is a powerful ORM (Object-Relational Mapping) tool for handling relational databases. It's designed to be developer-friendly and abstracts common database operations (like inserts, queries, updates, and deletes) to reduce the amount of boilerplate code developers must write.

Messaging and Stream Processing

In the realm of messaging and event-driven architectures, Go developers often turn to libraries like **`nsq`** or brokers like Apache Kafka. **`Nsq`** is a real-time distributed messaging platform designed to operate at scale, handling billions of messages per day. It's easy to set up and integrates well with existing Go applications, making it a popular choice for microservices architectures that require robust, low-latency messaging.

Apache Kafka, another high-throughput distributed messaging system, has strong support in the Go ecosystem through libraries like **`confluent-kafka-go`** or **`sarama`**. These libraries allow Go applications to produce and consume messages efficiently, facilitating the building of complex processing pipelines that are scalable and resilient.

Security and Authentication

For security and authentication, libraries like **`golang.org/x/oauth2`** provide OAuth2 functionality, which is crucial for modern web applications. JSON Web Tokens (JWT) can be managed using the **`dgrijalva/jwt-go`** library, which facilitates token creation, parsing, and validation, securing the application endpoints.

Containerization and Virtualization

Docker is a pivotal part of modern backend infrastructure, allowing applications to run in controlled environments. The **`docker`** SDK for Go allows developers to interact with Docker, automating tasks such as container management, image manipulation, and orchestration directly from Go applications.

Networking and Protocols

On the networking front, Go supports advanced TCP, UDP, and HTTP server capabilities natively. For microservices and inter-service communication, **`grpc-go`** provides a framework for RPC (Remote Procedure Calls) development, leveraging HTTP/2 for fast communication between services.

Testing and Deployment

Testing frameworks like **`go test`** are part of the Go toolchain, offering a cohesive methodology for unit and benchmark testing. Tools such as **`delve`** provide debugging capabilities, essential for developing complex applications.

Each of the aforementioned libraries and components serves a distinct purpose in strengthening the capacity to efficiently construct, safeguard, validate, and expand backend systems.

Installing Go

With Go's easy installation on Linux, you can take use of all the strong capabilities it offers for backend development. To ensure that everything in this book is up to date, we will install Go version 1.18 for all code examples and dependencies.

Preparation and Download

Before installing Go, you'll need to ensure your Linux system meets the necessary prerequisites. Most modern Linux distributions will already have these in place, but it's good to check and install any missing software:

- **GCC or Clang**: These compilers are essential for building packages that include C or C++ code. You can install GCC on Ubuntu with the command **`sudo apt install build-essential`**.
- **Curl or Wget**: These tools are useful for downloading files from the command line. You can install Curl on Ubuntu with **`sudo apt install curl`**.

- **Unzip and Tar**: These are required to unpack the Go binary. Install them on Ubuntu with **sudo apt install tar**.

Once you have the prerequisites sorted, the next step is to download the Go binary. Navigate to the official Go downloads page at **https://golang.org/dl/** using a web browser or a command-line tool like **wget** or **curl**. For Go 1.18, locate the Linux binary file, which typically ends with **.tar.gz**. Given below is how you might download it using **curl**:

```
curl -LO https://golang.org/dl/go1.18.linux-amd64.tar.gz
```

Installation

After downloading, you will install Go by extracting the binary into the appropriate directory. The conventional location to install Go is **/usr/local/go**. This location is preferred because it avoids conflict with system packages and can be accessed by multiple users. To proceed with the installation, use the following commands:

```
sudo tar -C /usr/local -xzf go1.18.linux-amd64.tar.gz
```

The above command extracts the Go archive to **/usr/local**, creating a **go** directory with all necessary files.

Setting up the Environment

For Go to function properly on your system, you need to configure the environment variables. The most critical variables are **GOROOT**, **GOPATH**, and **PATH**.

- GOROOT is the location where Go is installed. If you followed the standard installation steps, this would be **/usr/local/go**. However, modern Go distributions set this variable automatically, so you might not need to explicitly set it anymore.
- GOPATH is your workspace directory. It is where Go will download and install additional packages. While Go modules have made **GOPATH** less critical, it is still used for storing globally installed packages and binaries. A good place for **GOPATH** is your home directory. Following is how to set it:

```
export GOPATH=$HOME/go
```

- You need to add the Go binary directory to your **PATH** to run Go commands from any terminal. Add the following line to your shell's profile file (e.g., **.bashrc**, **.bash_profile**, or **.profile**):

```
export PATH=$PATH:/usr/local/go/bin:$GOPATH/bin
```

After adding these lines to your profile, source the file to apply the changes:

```
source ~/.bashrc
```

Verification

To verify that Go is installed correctly on your system, you can use the **`go version`** command, which should output the version of Go that is currently installed:

```
go version
```

If everything is configured correctly, it should display:

```
go version go1.18 linux/amd64
```

Now that Go is set up and installed, you can begin using it to create and execute Go programs. Try creating a simple "Hello, World" program to ensure everything is working as expected. Create a file named **`hello.go`** with the following Go code:

```
package main


import "fmt"


func main() {
 fmt.Println("Hello, World!")
}
```

Run the program using:

```
go run hello.go
```

The above command compiles and executes the Go program, and you should see **`Hello, World!`** printed in the terminal. This confirms that your Go installation is ready, and you can proceed with developing more complex Go applications as learned in subsequent chapters.

Setting up Visual Studio Code

To maximize efficiency and improve your coding experience, you should configure Visual Studio Code (VS Code) with the right extensions and settings for Go programming. After installing Go, as previously described, the following step is to configure VS Code to efficiently manage Go projects.

Installing VS Code and Go Extension

First, ensure that VS Code is installed on your Linux system. If it is not already installed, you can download it from the official VS Code website and follow the installation instructions provided there.

Once VS Code is installed, the essential step for Go development is installing the Go extension from the VS Code Marketplace. The Go extension, officially supported by the Go team at Google, provides features like IntelliSense, code navigation, and code editing support.

To install the extension:

- Open VS Code.
- Go to the Extensions view by clicking on the square icon on the sidebar or pressing **`Ctrl+Shift+X`**.
- Search for "Go" and find the extension by Google.
- Click on the install button.

This extension automatically configures itself to use the **`go`** binary in your system's path. It also suggests tools to install that enhance the coding experience, such as **`gopls`**, the Go language server, which offers capabilities like auto-completion, go-to-definition, and automatic imports.

Configuring Go Extension

After installation, some configurations can be adjusted to tailor the environment to your needs. For instance, you might want to configure the extension to format your code automatically on save or to adjust the settings for code linting.

You can access these settings by:

- Opening the Command Palette with **`Ctrl+Shift+P`**.
- Typing **`Preferences: Open Settings (UI)`** and hitting Enter.
- Searching for "Go" or directly editing settings related to formatting or linting under the

Extensions > Go configuration section.

There are still few more specific settings to consider:

- **`go.formatTool`**: This setting specifies which formatting tool to use. The default is **`gofmt`**, which is widely used in the Go community.
- **`go.useLanguageServer`**: Set this to **`true`** to enable the use of **`gopls`**, which provides enhanced language features.
- **`go.lintTool`**: Specifies the linter tool. Popular options include **`golint`** and **`staticcheck`**.

Setting up the Workspace

Once Visual Studio Code and the Go plugin are prepared, you may arrange your workspace as follows:

- Open the folder where you will be working on your Go projects by using **`File > Open Folder`** and selecting your Go workspace, which you might have set as **GOPATH** in your earlier Go setup.
- To ensure that VS Code recognizes this folder as a Go workspace, you can create a simple Go file (e.g., **`main.go`**) and open it. VS Code and the Go extension will detect the Go environment and automatically offer to install any missing dependencies.

Debugging Setup

To set up debugging:

- Ensure that the **`delve`** debugger is installed. If not already installed, the Go extension in VS Code might prompt you to install it.
- In VS Code, switch to the debug view by clicking on the play icon in the sidebar or pressing **`Ctrl+Shift+D`**.
- Click on "create a launch.json file" then select "Go" to auto-generate a debug configuration file. This file defines how the Go programs are launched and debugged.

Following is an example of a simple **`launch.json`** for a basic Go application:

```
{
 "version": "0.2.0",
 "configurations": [
```

```
{
"name": "Launch",
"type": "go",
"request": "launch",
"program": "${workspaceFolder}/main.go",
"env": {},
"args": []
}
]
}
```

This configuration will start the debugger for the Go file you are currently focused on.

Testing Integration

To run tests within VS Code, you can use the built-in support from the Go extension. It detects Go test files (**`*_test.go`**) and provides a UI to run and debug tests directly from the editor. Icons appear near the test functions to run or debug tests individually or file-wide.

If you follow the instructions carefully, this whole VS Code configuration will not only allow writing and navigating code, but will also include vital tools for formatting, linting, debugging, and testing, all of which are critical components of any development workflow.

Go Modules for Package Management

The Go ecosystem would not be complete without Go modules, which offer a robust method for handling dependencies. After making an experimental debut in Go 1.11, modules quickly became the de facto norm for package management, supplanting the old GOPATH-based approach. The newly developed approach addresses numerous difficulties, including package repeatability and dependency versioning, both of which are familiar to Go developers.

What are Go Modules?

A Go module is essentially a collection of Go packages stored in a file tree with a **go.mod** file at its root. The **go.mod** file defines the module's dependencies, including specific versions, which allows for more predictable builds. This predictability is crucial for large-scale projects like our example project, **gitforgits.com**, where managing the exact versions of dependencies ensures that the application behaves consistently across different environments.

Setting up New Module

To demonstrate the use of Go modules, we set up a new project for **gitforgits.com**. First, create a directory for your project:

```
mkdir gitforgits

cd gitforgits
```

Inside this directory, initialize a new module:

```
go mod init gitforgits.com
```

This command creates a **go.mod** file in your project directory. This file will track your dependencies.

Adding Dependencies

When you import packages in your Go code that are not part of the standard library, Go modules will automatically find and record the appropriate versions of these dependencies in your **go.mod** file. For instance, if your project needs the popular web framework **Gin**, you would import it in your Go code:

```
import "github.com/gin-gonic/gin"
```

Then run:

```
go build
```

or

```
go test
```

These commands will automatically add **Gin** to your **go.mod** file and download the dependency into your project's local cache. Given below is what your **go.mod** file might look like after adding

Gin:

```
module gitforgits.com

go 1.18

require github.com/gin-gonic/gin v1.7.4
```

Understanding go.mod File

The **go.mod** file consists of several parts:

- The **module** statement defines the module's name, which is usually the repository location where your module can be found.
- The **go** statement specifies the Go version used in this module.
- The **require** section lists the direct dependencies along with their versions.
- Optionally, a **replace** directive can be used to replace a dependency with another version or a local path. This is particularly useful for local development or when needing to fork a module.
- The **exclude** directive can exclude specific versions of a dependency.

Using go.sum File

Alongside the **go.mod** file, Go also maintains a **go.sum** file. This file contains the expected cryptographic checksums of the content of specific versions of dependencies. The **go.sum** file provides an extra layer of validation to ensure that the dependencies your module uses have not been tampered with. When you run **go mod tidy**, Go updates the **go.mod** and **go.sum** files to ensure they reflect all the modules your project depends on and removes unnecessary ones.

We will assume **gitforgits.com** needs a specific version of a library for handling OAuth, such as **golang.org/x/oauth2**. To add this library, specify it in your imports, and Go will handle the rest:

```
import "golang.org/x/oauth2/google"
```

After running **go build** or **go test**, the dependency is recorded in **go.mod**:

```
require golang.org/x/oauth2 v0.0.0-20220525143415-
9dcd33a902f4
```

This ensures that everyone working on the **gitforgits.com** project uses the exact same version of the OAuth library, thus avoiding "it works on my machine" issues.

Managing Upgrades and Downgrades

Managing dependencies also involves upgrading or downgrading to different versions. This is done using commands like:

```
go get golang.org/x/oauth2@latest
```

or specifying a specific version:

```
go get golang.org/x/oauth2@v0.0.0-20220426230321-
2e8d93401602
```

After running these commands, the **go.mod** and **go.sum** files will be updated accordingly. The use of modules makes your project more maintainable and reproducible by allowing you to control the updates to dependencies. Without having to worry about the nitty-gritty of package versions and compatibility, developers can put more effort into creating their applications with this system.

Basics of a Go program

Before beginning to build the robust backend services for our example project, **gitforgits.com**, it is essential for any developer to understand the basics of a Go program. The efficiency and readability of the Go programming language are based on a small set of fundamental ideas and syntax rules.

Basic Structure of a Go Program

Every Go program starts with a package declaration, which defines the namespace in which the code resides. The most common package is **main**, indicating that the package should compile as an executable program rather than a shared library.

Following is the basic skeleton of a Go program:

```
package main
```

```
import (
 "fmt"
)

func main() {
 fmt.Println("Hello, gitforgits.com")
}
```

In the above script,

- **Package Declaration**: **`package main`** - This line declares that the file belongs to the main package, and it's the starting point for the application.
- **Import Statement**: **`import "fmt"`** - This line tells the Go compiler to include the code from the **`fmt`** package, which contains functions for formatting text, including printing to the console.
- **Functions**: The **`func main()`** declaration starts the definition of a function. In Go, **`main.main()`** is the entry point of an executable program (not libraries). The **`fmt.Println()`** function inside **`main`** is used to print text to the standard output.

Variables and Types

Go is a statically typed language, which means you must declare the type of a variable. Given below is how you declare variables in Go:

```
var name string = "gitforgits.com"
var visitors int = 1000
```

However, Go also supports type inference with the **`:=`** syntax, allowing you to declare a variable without explicitly stating the type:

```
name := "gitforgits.com"
visitors := 1000
```

Control Structures

Go has several control structures familiar to users of C-like languages, including **`if`**, **`else`**, **`for`**, and **`switch`**.

If statement

```
if visitors > 1000 {

 fmt.Println("High traffic")

} else {

 fmt.Println("Normal traffic")

}
```

For loop

```
for i := 0; i < 10; i++ {

 fmt.Println("Visitor number", i+1)

}
```

Switch statement

```
switch day := 4; day {

case 1:

 fmt.Println("Monday")

case 2:

 fmt.Println("Tuesday")

case 3:

 fmt.Println("Wednesday")
```

```
case 4:
 fmt.Println("Thursday")
default:
 fmt.Println("Another day")
}
```

Arrays, Slices, and Maps

Arrays

```
var scores [10]int // an array of ten integers
```

Slices

They are more flexible than arrays; they do not require you to declare a fixed size:

```
visitors := []int{250, 320, 280, 300}
visitors = append(visitors, 350)
```

Maps

```
visitorCounts := map[string]int{"Monday": 300, "Tuesday": 450}
visitorCounts["Wednesday"] = 500
```

Functions

Functions in Go are declared using the **func** keyword. They can take parameters and return results. Given below is a simple function:

```
func greet(name string) string {
 return "Hello, " + name
}
```

```go
func main() {
 message := greet("gitforgits.com visitors")
 fmt.Println(message)
}
```

Concurrency with Goroutines

Go's real power lies in its built-in support for concurrency. You can create concurrent functions simply by prefixing a function call with **go**:

```go
go process(visitorData)
```

To handle synchronization and communication between goroutines, Go uses channels:

```go
func report(done chan bool) {
 fmt.Println("Preparing report for gitforgits.com")
 done <- true // Send a value to indicate completion
}


func main() {
 done := make(chan bool, 1)
 go report(done)
 <-done // Wait for the report to be finished
 fmt.Println("Report finished")
}
```

As we go further into the project, we may construct more intricate backend logic using the core concepts of Go programming, including variables, control structures, and goroutines.

Introduction to 'gitforgits.com' Project

As a case study for our practical learning, we have created a made-up online bookstore called gitforgits.com. As we go into backend development, this project will serve as a practical case study. We can apply our Go programming expertise in a real-world context because it will incorporate functionality seen in e-commerce systems.

Project Overview

`gitforgits.com` aims to provide a seamless and efficient online book purchasing experience. The primary features of the website include listing books, user registration and authentication, a shopping cart, and a checkout process with order management.

Functional Requirements

- **User Registration and Authentication**: Users must be able to register on the platform and log in. The system will handle authentication and maintain user sessions to keep users logged in while they browse books.
- **Product Listing**: The site will list books that users can browse. Each book will have details like title, author, price, and a short description. The backend will retrieve this data from a database.
- **Search Functionality**: Users will be able to search for books based on different criteria such as title, author, or genre.
- **Shopping Cart**: Users can add books to a virtual shopping cart, adjust quantities, or remove items from the cart.
- **Checkout Process**: The checkout feature will collect user shipping information and payment details. For simplicity, payment processing will be simulated.
- **Order Management**: After a purchase, the user's order details (such as items, quantities, prices, and delivery status) will be recorded and retrievable by the user.
- **Administration Panel**: There will be functionalities for site administrators to add, update, or remove book listings, view orders, and manage users.

Technical Requirements

- **Backend**: The backend of `gitforgits.com` will be developed entirely in Go, using Go's standard library and additional frameworks and libraries where appropriate.

- **Frontend**: The frontend may be simple, as the focus is on backend development. Basic HTML and JavaScript might be used for demonstration purposes.
- **Database**: A relational database will store user and product information. MySQL or PostgreSQL could be used depending on the requirements for complexity.
- **Concurrency Handling**: The backend will handle concurrent users efficiently, using Go's goroutines and channels to manage multiple users interacting with the website at the same time.
- **Security**: Basic security measures will be implemented, including secure password storage, HTTPS for secure communications, and protection against common vulnerabilities like SQL injection and Cross-Site Scripting (XSS).
- **APIs**: RESTful APIs will be developed for handling frontend requests like adding items to the cart, checking out, and user registration.
- **Deployment**: The application will be containerized using Docker for easy deployment and scalability.

Design Considerations

- **Modular Architecture**: The backend will be structured in a modular fashion, separating concerns and making the system easier to manage and scale. For instance, authentication, product management, and order processing might each be a separate module.
- **State Management**: Given the need for session management in e-commerce platforms, careful consideration will be given to how user state is maintained across the user's journey on the site.
- **Performance Optimization**: Performance will be a key consideration, especially for database interactions and API response times. The design will include efficient querying and data handling strategies to ensure a smooth user experience.
- **Scalability**: As **`gitforgits.com`** is envisioned as a platform that could scale to handle a significant load of user traffic and data, its architecture will support scaling, particularly through the use of microservices where necessary.

Quick Project Code Structure

To start with, the below is a simple Go code snippet showing how one might define a basic structure for a book and a function to fetch book details:

```
package main
```

```
import (
 "fmt"
)

type Book struct {
 ID int
 Title string
 Author string
 Description string
 Price float64
}

func getBookDetails(id int) *Book {
 // Simulate fetching a book from a database
 return &Book{
 ID: id,
 Title: "Sample Book",
 Author: "John Doe",
 Description: "A fascinating exploration of Go
programming.",
 Price: 29.99,
 }
```

```
}


func main() {
 book := getBookDetails(1)
 fmt.Printf("Book: %+v\n", book)
}
```

The application will build on this code, which illustrates the core approach to constructing Go data structures and basic functions. Moving ahead, we want to increase the application's functionality by leveraging Go's capabilities to address real-world backend development difficulties.

Git for Version Control

Git is an indispensable tool for managing software development initiatives, including gitforgits.com, as it is a distributed version control system. It allows several programmers to work on a single project without producing disputes, and the codebase can be monitored for each change, making rollbacks and version tracking considerably easier.

Why use Git?

Using Git for **`gitforgits.com`** enables the team to:

- Track changes in the project files.
- Collaborate with others seamlessly, merging changes from multiple developers.
- Maintain a history of who made what changes and when.
- Revert to previous versions of the project if a problem is detected in the current version.
- Manage different versions and branches of the project, allowing experimental development without affecting the main codebase.

Basic Git Commands

To get started with Git, first, you need to install it on your machine. Once installed, you can configure it with your information, which will be used in your commits:

```
git config --global user.name "Your Name"

git config --global user.email
"your.email@gitforgits.com"
```

For **gitforgits.com**, the first step after setting up the directory (as previously learned) is to initialize a new Git repository:

```
git init
```

The above command creates a new **.git** directory in your project folder, where all the project's version history will be stored.

Adding Files and Committing Changes

Once your Git repository is initialized, you can start adding files to the project. For instance, after creating a new file like **main.go**, you need to add it to the repository:

```
git add main.go
```

To save the changes, you need to commit them:

```
git commit -m "Initial commit with main.go"
```

The **-m** flag allows you to add a commit message, a brief description of what changes were made in that commit.

Branching

Branching is a powerful feature in Git that lets you diverge from the main line of development and continue to work independently without affecting the main project. For example, if you want to develop a new feature for **gitforgits.com**, you can create a new branch:

```
git branch feature-new-checkout-system

git checkout feature-new-checkout-system
```

Or in a single command with newer versions of Git:

```
git checkout -b feature-new-checkout-system
```

This creates a new branch and switches to it. Changes made and committed on this branch do not affect the main branch (**`master`** or **`main`**), allowing for safe development and experimentation.

Viewing Changes and Logs

To see what has changed in your files:

```
git status
```

The above command shows which files have changed and which files are staged for a commit. If you want to see the exact changes made, you can use:

```
git diff
```

To view the commit history:

```
git log
```

This command shows a list of all commits in the current branch, along with their IDs, author information, and commit messages.

Merging Branches

After development of a feature is complete on a branch, it can be merged back into the main branch. For example, once the new checkout system is tested and ready to be part of the main application, you would switch back to the main branch and merge the feature branch:

```
git checkout main

git merge feature-new-checkout-system
```

This command incorporates changes from **`feature-new-checkout-system`** into the **`main`** branch.

Handling Merge Conflicts

Sometimes, Git cannot automatically merge changes, resulting in conflicts. You will need to manually resolve these by editing the files shown by Git and then marking them as resolved:

```
git add filename
```

After resolving conflicts, you can continue the merging process.

Using Git with Remote Repositories

For collaborative projects like **gitforgits.com**, you'll likely use a remote repository (like those hosted on GitHub, GitLab, or Bitbucket). To sync your local repository with a remote repository:

```
git remote add origin
https://github.com/username/gitforgits.com.git

git push -u origin main
```

This sets up a remote named **origin** linked to your repository URL, and pushes your commits to it.

Docker Basics

Docker is a platform that uses containerization technology to facilitate application deployment within containers. This platform guarantees that the program will run flawlessly in every environment, whether it is a personal laptop, a test server, or a production system. To avoid the normal "it works on my machine" issue with our project, gitforgits.com, we must create a development environment that matches production, and understanding the fundamentals of Docker is required.

What are Docker Containers?

Software code, libraries, configuration files, environment variables, and runtime are all contained in small, standalone executable packages called containers. Containers are segregated from one another and the host system, yet they share the OS kernel, start quickly, and consume less CPU and RAM.

Images and Containers

The fundamental concepts in Docker are images and containers. A Docker image is a snapshot of a container, a static specification of what the program needs to run. On the other hand, a container is a runtime instance of an image—what the image becomes in memory when executed.

Dockerfile

To create a Docker image, you start with a base image and use a Dockerfile. A Dockerfile is a text document that contains all the commands a user could call on the command line to assemble an image. For instance, to build a simple Docker image for the **gitforgits.com** application, you might start with a basic Go image and then copy your application code into the image:

```
# Use the official Go runtime as a parent image
FROM golang:1.18


# Set the working directory
WORKDIR /go/src/app


# Copy the current directory contents into the container
at /go/src/app
COPY . .


# Download all the dependencies
RUN go get -d -v ./...


# Install the package
RUN go install -v ./...


# Make port 80 available to the world outside this
container
EXPOSE 80


# Run the executable
```

```
CMD ["app"]
```

This Dockerfile starts with a Go image, sets the working directory, copies the application directory from your project into the Docker image, installs dependencies, exposes port 80, and specifies the command to run the application.

Building and Running Docker Containers

Once you have a Dockerfile, you can build the image using:

```
docker build -t gitforgits.com .
```

The above command tells Docker to build an image from the Dockerfile in the current directory and tag this image with the name **gitforgits.com**.

After building the image, you can run it in a container:

```
docker run -p 4000:80 gitforgits.com
```

The above command runs the image as a container, mapping port 80 of the container to port 4000 on your host, allowing you to access the application via **localhost:4000** in your web browser.

Docker Compose

For more complex applications like **gitforgits.com**, which might require running multiple containers (e.g., one for the application server, another for the database), Docker Compose is used. Docker Compose is a tool for defining and running multi-container Docker applications. With Compose, you use a YAML file to configure your application's services, networks, and volumes.

Following is an example of a **docker-compose.yml** file for **gitforgits.com**:

```
version: '3'

services:

 web:

 build: .

 ports:
```

```
- "4000:80"
db:
image: postgres
environment:
POSTGRES_DB: gitforgits
POSTGRES_USER: user
POSTGRES_PASSWORD: password
```

This configuration defines two services: **web**, which builds from the current directory, and **db**, which uses a pre-built PostgreSQL image. It also sets up environment variables for the database, such as the database name, user, and password.

Starting and Managing Project Containers

With Docker Compose, you can start all services defined in your **docker-compose.yml** with one command:

```
docker-compose up
```

And you can stop them with:

```
docker-compose down
```

Volumes and Networks

To persist data and manage the network between containers, Docker allows you to define volumes and networks. In the **docker-compose.yml** file, you can specify volumes to persist the database data and custom networks to facilitate communication between containers.

The above well-introduced Docker covers all the essentials you need to know to begin incorporating this technology into your development projects with ease.

Summary

We started by going over the basics of the Go programming language, focusing on how well it works and how well it fits the bill for creating solid backend systems. We gave an overview of the Go ecosystem, highlighting libraries and tools that are useful for backend development, such as gorilla/mux for routing, gorm for object relationship management, and nsq for message brokers. To keep things consistent, we went over how to install Go in depth and made sure to use Go 1.18 in all of our examples.

After that, we used VS Code to set up the development environment, adding the required Go extensions to make coding easier and more productive. The importance of Go modules in package management was learned, with a focus on how they facilitate efficient dependency management. We also went over the components and syntax of a Go program, illustrating their practical application with our sample book selling platform, gitforgits.com. Writing functions, managing imports, and using variables were some of the fundamentals of Go project setup that we covered.

Last but not least, we learned Git version control and its significance in managing project versions and team collaboration. At the end, we covered the basics of Docker and how containerization can be used to maintain consistent environments across development and production.

CHAPTER 2: BUILDING A BASIC WEB SERVER WITH NET/HTTP

Chapter Overview

This chapter looks into the practical elements of utilizing Go's net/http package to create a simple web server, which is a fundamental skill for backend engineers. We will begin by looking at the capabilities and key components of the net/http package, which includes the tools needed to build HTTP servers and process web requests successfully. As we go, you will learn how to configure your own web server, including the basics of launching a server and handling basic HTTP requests.

The chapter continues by breaking down the structure of HTTP requests and answers, shedding light on the data exchange process between a server and a client. We will go over how to use http.ServeMux, Go's default multiplexer, to route requests to the appropriate handlers, allowing you to manage many URLs and pathways easily.

For the purpose of building RESTful APIs, next steps will focus on managing various HTTP methods, including GET, POST, PUT, and DELETE, among many others. You'll also learn how to employ query parameters and URL fragments to obtain information given by clients, which is required for dynamic answers based on user input. We will go over the steps to set up your Go server to serve static files and assets, which are an essential part of any web server. This will allow your server to run a full-fledged web application by serving HTML, CSS, and JavaScript.

Finally, the chapter will walk you through the best ways to structure a Go web application project. This involves structuring your code, managing dependencies, and creating a project environment that can scale as your application grows. By the end of this chapter, you'll have a strong grasp of how to design and manage simple web servers in Go, as well as the ability to develop more complex backend systems.

Introduction to 'net/http' Package

The **`net/http`** package is a robust toolset that allows developers to build and handle HTTP servers and clients. It forms the backbone of web communications in many Go applications, including our example project for **`gitforgits.com`**. Understanding this package is crucial for any backend developer who intends to implement web services and APIs efficiently.

Core Components of net/http

At its core, the **`net/http`** package provides a set of interfaces and functions that manage server and client communications over HTTP. The primary components include:

1. **HTTP Client**: The package includes capabilities to create HTTP clients, which are essential for making requests to external HTTP servers. This is typically used for calling APIs, fetching data from external resources, or interacting with other microservices.
2. **HTTP Server**: This component allows you to build HTTP servers. You can define your

server's behavior to listen for HTTP requests on any port, and handle these requests using handler functions.

3. **Request and Response Types:** **`http.Request`** and **`http.Response`** are struct types that represent HTTP requests and responses, respectively. A **`Request`** object holds all the information about an incoming request (like URL, headers, body, etc.), while a **`Response`** object is what your server needs to send back to the client.

4. **Handlers and ServeMux:** Handlers are objects that handle an HTTP request and are represented by the **`http.Handler`** interface, which requires a method **`ServeHTTP`**. The **`http.ServeMux`** (or multiplexer) is a router that directs requests to different handlers based on the URL path.

Working with HTTP Servers

To set up a basic HTTP server, you define a handler function or method that implements the **`http.Handler`** interface, and then attach this handler to a server instance.

Given below is a simple example:

```
package main


import (
 "fmt"
 "net/http"
)


func helloWorld(w http.ResponseWriter, r *http.Request) {
 fmt.Fprintf(w, "Hello, World!")
}


func main() {
```

```
 http.HandleFunc("/", helloWorld)

 http.ListenAndServe(":8080", nil)

}
```

In the above code snippet, the **helloWorld** function is set as the handler for the root URL. When a web browser requests the root URL, it receives "Hello, World!" as a response. The **http.ListenAndServe** function tells your application to listen on port 8080 and handle requests using handlers set up via **http.HandleFunc**.

Deep Dive into HTTP Handlers

Handlers are central to processing HTTP requests. They take two parameters: an **http.ResponseWriter** and an **http.Request**. The **ResponseWriter** is used to write a response back to the client, including setting response headers and writing the response body. The **Request** contains all the data about the request from the client, including URL, query parameters, headers, and the body.

For more control, you can define types that implement the **http.Handler** interface. This approach is helpful for structuring larger applications or when more functionality than a simple function is needed:

```
type MessageHandler struct {

 Message string

}


func (m *MessageHandler) ServeHTTP(w http.ResponseWriter,
r *http.Request) {

 fmt.Fprintf(w, m.Message)

}


func main() {
```

```
 messageHandler := &MessageHandler{Message: "Hello,
gitforgits.com"}
 http.Handle("/", messageHandler)
 http.ListenAndServe(":8080", nil)
}
```

This structure allows you to configure the handler with specific data, in this case, a message to display.

Understanding Request and Response

In any HTTP interaction, understanding the structure of requests and responses is vital. The **`http.Request`** object provides access to the data in an HTTP request:

- **`Method`**: Specifies the HTTP method (GET, POST, etc.).
- **`URL`**: Contains the URL being requested.
- **`Header`**: A map containing the HTTP headers.
- **`Body`**: The body of the request, which can be read using standard Go I/O libraries (**`io`**).

The **`http.ResponseWriter`** is used to build the HTTP response:

- Writing to **`w`** writes the data to the body of the response.
- The **`Header()`** method returns the headers map to modify the response's headers.
- **`WriteHeader(statusCode int)`** sets the HTTP status code for the response.

The **`net/http`** package contains complete tools for developing HTTP servers and clients, allowing Go developers to easily handle routing, manage requests and answers, and implement required web server capabilities. Building scalable and reliable backend services requires a solid grasp of this package, as demonstrated on gitforgits.com.

Creating your first web server

- An essential initial step in developing the infrastructure for **`gitforgits.com`** is to launch your very own web server with the help of the **`net/http`** package. This server will serve as the backbone for our bookselling platform, processing all HTTP requests. We will follow a step-by-step instruction to set up this server, including how to handle basic routing and react to HTTP requests.

Setup Basic HTTP Server

The first step in creating your web server is to write a simple Go program that listens for HTTP requests on a specified port. Given below is how you can do it:

```
package main


import (
 "fmt"
 "net/http"
)


func main() {
 http.HandleFunc("/", func(w http.ResponseWriter, r
*http.Request) {
 fmt.Fprintf(w, "Welcome to gitforgits.com!")
 })


 fmt.Println("Server starting on port 8080...")
 if err := http.ListenAndServe(":8080", nil); err != nil
{
 fmt.Println("Error starting server: ", err)
 return
 }
}
```

In this code:

- **`http.HandleFunc`** is used to add a route handler for the root URL (**"/"**). Whenever HTTP requests are made to the root URL, the provided function is called.
- The function takes two parameters: **`http.ResponseWriter`** (to write the response back to the client) and **`*http.Request`** (which contains all information about the request).
- **`http.ListenAndServe`** starts an HTTP server with a given address (in this case, port 8080) and handler (in this case, **`nil`**, which means using the default multiplexer provided by **`http`**).

Handling Different Routes

The next step is to add more features so that users may access different sections of the website through multiple pathways. For instance, implementing a route to display a list of books may look like this:

```
func booksHandler(w http.ResponseWriter, r *http.Request)
{

 fmt.Fprintf(w, "Here are the available books.")

}



func main() {

 http.HandleFunc("/", func(w http.ResponseWriter, r
*http.Request) {

 fmt.Fprintf(w, "Welcome to gitforgits.com!")

 })

 http.HandleFunc("/books", booksHandler)



 fmt.Println("Server starting on port 8080...")
```

```
 if err := http.ListenAndServe(":8080", nil); err != nil
{
 fmt.Println("Error starting server: ", err)
 return
 }
}
```

In the above script,

- A new handler function **booksHandler** is defined, which will handle requests to **/books**.
- **http.HandleFunc("/books", booksHandler)** maps the **/books** path to the **booksHandler** function.

Handling HTTP Methods

Web applications often need to respond differently based on the HTTP method (GET, POST, PUT, DELETE). Following is how to modify a handler to check the method of the request:

```
func booksHandler(w http.ResponseWriter, r *http.Request)
{
 switch r.Method {
 case "GET":
 fmt.Fprintf(w, "Showing books")
 case "POST":
 fmt.Fprintf(w, "Adding a new book")
 default:
 http.Error(w, "Unsupported method",
http.StatusMethodNotAllowed)
```

```
 }
}
```

This above script,

- Uses a **switch** statement on **r.Method** to differentiate between GET and POST methods.
- Returns an error for methods that are not supported.

Query Parameters and URL Fragments

You may make your server more dynamic by handling query parameters. For example, to sort books by genre:

```
func booksHandler(w http.ResponseWriter, r *http.Request)
{
 switch r.Method {
 case "GET":
 genre := r.URL.Query().Get("genre")
 if genre != "" {
 fmt.Fprintf(w, "Showing books from genre: %s", genre)
 } else {
 fmt.Fprintf(w, "Showing all books")
 }
 case "POST":
 fmt.Fprintf(w, "Adding a new book")
 default:
 http.Error(w, "Unsupported method",
http.StatusMethodNotAllowed)
```

```
    }
}
```

In this script,

- **`r.URL.Query().Get("genre")`** extracts the value of the **`genre`** parameter from the URL query string.
- The server responds differently based on whether the **`genre`** parameter is present.

Running and Testing Server

To see your server in action, run your Go program. Open a web browser or use a tool like **`curl`** to make requests to **`http://localhost:8080/`** and **`http://localhost:8080/books?genre=fiction`**. You should see the responses based on the logic you've coded.

This methodical approach provides a strong foundation for building further online features for **`gitforgits.com`**. As you develop, you will build on this foundation by including database interactions, user authentication, and increasingly advanced business logic.

Understanding Request and Response Structures

In web development, understanding the anatomy of HTTP requests and responses is fundamental for effective server-side programming. In the context of our project **`gitforgits.com`**, this knowledge is essential for developing features like book listings, user registrations, and order processing. Now that we know how a Go web server handles HTTP requests and answers, let us have a look at their fundamental structures.

HTTP Request Structure

An HTTP request made to a server consists of several components that tell the server what it needs to do and how. Given below is a breakdown:

1. **Method**: The HTTP method (also called "verb") indicates the action to be performed. Common methods include GET (retrieve data), POST (submit data), PUT (update data), DELETE (remove data), among others. For example, retrieving a list of books from **`gitforgits.com`** would typically use a GET request.
2. **URL/URI**: The Uniform Resource Locator (URL) or Uniform Resource Identifier (URI) specifies the path or endpoint on the server. For instance, accessing

http://gitforgits.com/books might direct the server to handle requests related to books.

3. **HTTP Version**: This specifies the HTTP protocol version, such as HTTP/1.1 or HTTP/2, which informs the server about the capabilities of the client.
4. **Headers**: Request headers provide essential information about the request or about the client itself, such as **Content-Type** (the type of data being sent), **Authorization** (credentials for accessing resources), and many other possible fields that control the request or inform the server.
5. **Body**: Not all requests have a body. Bodies are primarily used with POST and PUT requests to send data to the server. For example, adding a new book on **gitforgits.com** would involve sending a POST request with the book details in the request body.

HTTP Response Structure

In response to an HTTP request, the server sends back an HTTP response, structured as follows:

1. **Status Line**: This includes the HTTP version, a status code, and a status message. The status code provides a quick indication of the result of the request, such as 200 (OK), 404 (Not Found), or 500 (Internal Server Error).
2. **Headers**: Response headers hold metadata about the response, such as **Content-Type** (what type of data is being returned), **Set-Cookie** (for setting cookies), and **Cache-Control** (instructions for caching the response).
3. **Body**: The response body contains the data requested by the client. For instance, a response to a request for a list of books might include JSON-formatted data detailing the books.

Flow of Request and Response

In order to better understand the flow, we look at a real-world example from our application that involves retrieving book details:

Client Request

- A user wants to view details about a book titled "Learning Go."
- The client sends a GET request to **http://gitforgits.com/books/123**, where "123" is the book ID.
- The request looks like this:
    - Method: GET

- URL: /books/123
- Headers: Accept: application/json

Server Handling

- The Go server's router (**`http.ServeMux`**) matches the path **`/books/123`** to a specific handler function.
- The handler function parses the URL to extract the book ID.
- It queries the database for the book ID, retrieves the book details, and prepares a JSON response.

Server Response

- Assuming the book is found, the server constructs an HTTP response:
  - Status Line: HTTP/1.1 200 OK
  - Headers: Content-Type: application/json
  - Body: **`{"id": "123", "title": "Learning Go", "author": "Jane Doe", "description": "An introductory book on Go programming."}`**

Client Receives

- The client receives the response, parses the JSON data, and displays the book details to the user.

Handling of Requests and Responses

Handling this flow involves several key steps:

- Parsing URL Path and Query Parameters: The **`http.Request`** object provides methods like **`URL.Path`** and **`URL.Query()`** which allow you to extract parts of the URL and query strings respectively.
- Reading the Body: For POST and PUT requests, you often need to read the body of the request. This is done using **`r.Body`**, an **`io.ReadCloser`**, which can be read like any other stream:

```
body, err := ioutil.ReadAll(r.Body)

if err != nil {
```

```
 http.Error(w, "Error reading body",
http.StatusBadRequest)

 return

}
```

- Setting Response Headers and Writing the Body: You set response headers using methods on **http.ResponseWriter**:

```
w.Header().Set("Content-Type", "application/json")

fmt.Fprint(w, jsonResponse)
```

This deep look at request and response architectures, combined with practical examples from gitforgits.com, demonstrated how web servers interpret and respond to client activities. To successfully manage client-server connections and guarantee appropriate processing and responses from the backend logic to different client requests, it is essential to understand this flow.

Basics of Routing with http.ServeMux

Routing is a fundamental aspect of any web application, directing incoming HTTP requests to the correct code that should handle them. In the context of our project, **gitforgits.com**, effective routing ensures that a request to view a book, add a book to the cart, or check out, all reach the appropriate functions that can execute these operations.

Understanding Routing

Routing is the process by which a web application handles different paths and methods on HTTP requests. When a user visits a URL or interacts with an application, the HTTP request's path and method need to be matched with specific code that can respond to it appropriately. For example, one URL might need to show a user their shopping cart, while another might handle the process of adding a new book.

Introduction to http.ServeMux

In Go, one of the simplest ways to handle routing is using the **http.ServeMux**, which is a multiplexer that matches the URL of each incoming request against a list of registered paths and calls the associated handler for the path whenever a match is found.

http.ServeMux is part of the **net/http** package and can be used to create new multiplexer instances or utilize the default multiplexer by calling functions directly from the package.

Features of http.ServeMux

- **Pattern Matching**: **http.ServeMux** matches the URL of a request against a list of registered patterns and executes the handler for the most specific matching pattern.
- **Clean URL Patterns**: It ensures that URL patterns are well-defined and can match exact tokens or prefixes.
- **Methods Are Ignored**: The multiplexer does not by default handle different methods differently; it purely matches based on the path.

Sample Program: Routing with http.ServeMux

We will write a simple Go program that uses **http.ServeMux** for routing different endpoints of our application **gitforgits.com**.

```
package main


import (
 "fmt"
 "net/http"
)


func mainHandler(w http.ResponseWriter, r *http.Request)
{
 fmt.Fprintf(w, "Welcome to gitforgits.com!")
}


func booksHandler(w http.ResponseWriter, r *http.Request)
```

```
{
 fmt.Fprintf(w, "Here are some books to browse.")
}

func orderHandler(w http.ResponseWriter, r *http.Request)
{
 fmt.Fprintf(w, "Here's your order summary.")
}

func main() {
 mux := http.NewServeMux()

 // Registering handlers
 mux.HandleFunc("/", mainHandler)
 mux.HandleFunc("/books", booksHandler)
 mux.HandleFunc("/order", orderHandler)

 // Starting the server
 fmt.Println("Server starting on port 8080...")
 if err := http.ListenAndServe(":8080", mux); err != nil
 {
 fmt.Println("Error starting server: ", err)
```

```
  }
}
```

In the above example,

- A new **ServeMux** instance is created.
- Three handlers are defined: one for the root path **/**, one for **/books**, and one for **/order**.
- Each handler function outputs a simple message that corresponds to its route.
- The **HandleFunc** method registers the handlers with the specific paths.
- **http.ListenAndServe** starts an HTTP server with the defined **ServeMux** as the handler, listening on port 8080.

When the server receives an HTTP request,

- The **ServeMux** checks the request URL against the list of registered patterns.
- It selects the handler for the most closely matching pattern. For instance, if the server receives a request for **/books**, it invokes the **booksHandler**.
- If no pattern is matched, **ServeMux** sends an HTTP 404 response.

An essential but simple aspect of developing a backend is learning how to use **http.ServeMux** for routing. It helps programmers organize their server's API in a sensible way, so the correct components can process the right kinds of requests. With the ever-changing nature of programs like **gitforgits.com**, this fundamental principle of web development becomes even more important for keeping code organized and efficient.

Handling Different HTTP Methods

Methods are commands that specify the action to be executed on a certain resource within the framework of Hypertext Transfer Protocol (HTTP) and web servers. To ensure that servers reply correctly according to the request's intent, each HTTP method has a predetermined role. To manage interactions like accessing book details, altering book information, or maintaining user sessions, **gitforgits.com** must comprehend and correctly implement these methods.

HTTP Methods

We will go over the different HTTP methods and how they work with some examples:

GET

The GET method requests a representation of the specified resource. It should only retrieve data and have no other effect.

```
func getBookHandler(w http.ResponseWriter, r
*http.Request) {

 fmt.Fprintf(w, "Retrieving book details.")

}
```

POST

The POST method submits data to be processed to a specified resource, often causing a change in state or side effects on the server.

```
func addBookHandler(w http.ResponseWriter, r
*http.Request) {

 fmt.Fprintf(w, "Adding a new book to the store.")

}
```

PUT

The PUT method replaces all current representations of the target resource with the request payload.

```
func updateBookHandler(w http.ResponseWriter, r
*http.Request) {

 fmt.Fprintf(w, "Updating an existing book's details.")

}
```

DELETE

The DELETE method deletes the specified resource.

```
func deleteBookHandler(w http.ResponseWriter, r
*http.Request) {
```

```
    fmt.Fprintf(w, "Deleting a book from the store.")
}
```

PATCH

The PATCH method is used to apply partial modifications to a resource.

```
func patchBookHandler(w http.ResponseWriter, r
*http.Request) {
    fmt.Fprintf(w, "Applying updates to a book's details.")
}
```

HEAD

The HEAD method is identical to GET except that the server must not return a message-body in the response. It is used for obtaining metadata.

```
func headBookHandler(w http.ResponseWriter, r
*http.Request) {
    w.Header().Set("Content-Length", "0")
}
```

OPTIONS

The OPTIONS method describes the communication options for the target resource.

```
func optionsHandler(w http.ResponseWriter, r
*http.Request) {
    w.Header().Set("Allow", "GET, POST, HEAD")
    fmt.Fprintf(w, "Provides options for the resource.")
}
```

TRACE

The TRACE method performs a message loop-back test along the path to the target resource, providing a diagnostic tool.

```
func traceHandler(w http.ResponseWriter, r *http.Request)
{

 fmt.Fprintf(w, "TRACE not implemented.")

}
```

CONNECT

The CONNECT method establishes a tunnel to the server identified by the target resource.

```
func connectHandler(w http.ResponseWriter, r
*http.Request) {

 fmt.Fprintf(w, "CONNECT not implemented.")

}
```

Sample Program: Implementing Handlers

To see these handlers in action, you can set up a basic server using **`http.ServeMux`**, registering each handler to a specific path and method:

```
func main() {

 mux := http.NewServeMux()


 mux.HandleFunc("/books", func(w http.ResponseWriter, r
*http.Request) {

  switch r.Method {

  case "GET":

  getBookHandler(w, r)
```

```
case "POST":
addBookHandler(w, r)
case "PUT":
updateBookHandler(w, r)
case "DELETE":
deleteBookHandler(w, r)
case "PATCH":
patchBookHandler(w, r)
case "HEAD":
headBookHandler(w, r)
case "OPTIONS":
optionsHandler(w, r)
case "TRACE":
traceHandler(w, r)
case "CONNECT":
connectHandler(w, r)
default:
http.Error(w, "Unsupported HTTP method",
http.StatusMethodNotAllowed)
}
})
```

```
 fmt.Println("Server starting on port 8080...")
 if err := http.ListenAndServe(":8080", mux); err != nil
{
 fmt.Println("Error starting server: ", err)
 }
}
```

This setup allows you to test each HTTP method's implementation by sending requests to the **/books** endpoint with different methods. The server will respond according to the logic defined in the corresponding handler, demonstrating the practical application of each HTTP method within the scope of your backend server for **gitforgits.com**.

Query Parameters and URL Fragments

The creation of dynamic and responsive web apps relies heavily on query parameters and fragments of URLs. They make it possible for servers to adapt their actions and content to the user's preferences by analyzing the data provided in the URL. This functionality is absolutely necessary for **gitforgits.com** because it allows users to do things like search, filter books, or jump to specific parts of a page.

Importance of Query Parameters and URL Fragments

Query Parameters

These are appended to the URL following a **?** and are used to store data that the client sends to the server.For example, in a URL like **http://gitforgits.com/books?genre=fiction**, the query parameter **genre=fiction** tells the server to filter the books displayed to those that match the genre 'fiction'. This makes the application interactive and capable of responding to user preferences without needing to hard code these preferences into the URL path.

URL Fragments

Fragments follow a **#** in the URL and are generally used to direct the browser to a specific section of the page without reloading the web page. For example, **http://gitforgits.com/books#author-details** might direct the user to the 'Author Details' section of the 'Books' page. Unlike query parameters, fragments are typically not sent to the server with the HTTP request; they are handled client-side by the browser.

Sample Program: Utilizing Query Parameters and URL Fragments

We will take a closer look at the Go backend for **gitforgits.com** and see how we can incorporate and use URL fragments and query parameters. We will concentrate on query parameters for server-side processing and touch on fragments briefly for client-side use.

Handling Query Parameters

Using query parameters allows the backend of **gitforgits.com** to handle requests dynamically. Suppose you want to implement a feature that lets users search for books by title or filter books by genre.

Given below is how you might set this up:

```
package main


import (
 "fmt"
 "net/http"
)


func booksHandler(w http.ResponseWriter, r *http.Request)
{
 // Parse query parameters
 title := r.URL.Query().Get("title")
 genre := r.URL.Query().Get("genre")


 response := "Books"
```

```
 if title != "" {
 response += fmt.Sprintf(" with title matching: %s",
title)
 }

 if genre != "" {
 response += fmt.Sprintf(" in genre: %s", genre)
 }

 fmt.Fprintf(w, response)
}

func main() {
 http.HandleFunc("/books", booksHandler)

 fmt.Println("Server starting on port 8080...")
 http.ListenAndServe(":8080", nil)
}
```

In the above sample program, the server extracts the **title** and **genre** parameters from the URL. If these parameters exist, the server includes them in the response, allowing the user to see a filtered list of books based on their query.

URL Fragments for Client-Side Handling

While Go does not directly handle URL fragments (since they are not sent to the server), it's useful to know how they might be used in conjunction with server-side setups. For instance, after a server response is rendered on a webpage, JavaScript running on the client's browser could take a fragment from the URL and use it to automatically scroll to a specific part of the page or to load additional data related to that fragment.

Testing Implementation

To test the above Go server code, you can use a web browser or tools like **curl** to send requests:

```
curl
"http://localhost:8080/books?title=Go%20Programming&genre
=Non-fiction"
```

This request would make the Go server respond with "Books with title matching: Go Programming in genre: Non-fiction", demonstrating how the server dynamically generates responses based on URL query parameters. Query parameters allow the server to tailor the data it sends back to the user, enabling functionalities such as search and filtering, which are essential for a data-rich application like an online bookstore. Meanwhile, URL fragments, though handled client-side, can enhance the user experience by guiding users directly to relevant sections of a webpage.

Serving Static Files and Assets

As with any web server, the backend of our book-selling platform, gitforgits.com, is responsible for serving static files and assets. Images, JavaScript scripts, Cascading Style Sheets (CSS), and HTML documents are examples of static files and assets. Web designers rely on these files to build the site's aesthetic and interactive components; however, they are not processed on the server before being sent to the client, which is why they are called "static."

Types of Static Files and Assets

1. **HTML Files**: These are the backbone of any web application, defining the structure of web pages.
2. **CSS Files**: Cascading Style Sheets define the layout and style of the HTML content, including colors, fonts, and spacing.
3. **JavaScript Files**: JavaScript files add interactivity to web pages, handling tasks like user input, data requests from the server without a page reload, and animations.
4. **Images**: Common formats include JPEG, PNG, GIF, and SVG. Images are used to enhance the visual appeal and convey information.

5. **Videos and Audio Files**: Media files can also be served statically, though they might require additional HTML5 tags for embedding.
6. **PDFs and Other Documents**: For a book selling site, serving static files might include digital downloads like PDFs or ePub files.

Serving Static Files

In Go, the **`net/http`** package provides a built-in way to serve static files using the **`http.FileServer`** handler, which serves a directory tree of static files. Given below is how you can set it up:

```
package main


import (
 "log"
 "net/http"
)


func main() {
 // Set the directory from which to serve static files.
 fs := http.FileServer(http.Dir("static"))


 // Handle all requests to the server's root path.
 http.Handle("/", fs)


 // Start the server on port 8080.
 log.Println("Serving on http://localhost:8080/")
```

```
err := http.ListenAndServe(":8080", nil)
if err != nil {
log.Fatal("ListenAndServe: ", err)
}
}
```

In the above code snippet,

- **http.Dir("static")** tells the **FileServer** to serve files out of the **static** directory relative to where the Go program is running. This directory should contain all your CSS, JavaScript, and image files.
- **http.Handle("/", fs)** sets up a handler that routes all web requests to the file server.

Structuring Static Directory

For organizational purposes, you might want to structure the **static** directory as follows:

```
/static
 /css
 - style.css
 /js
 - script.js
 /images
 - logo.png
 /pdf
 - sample.pdf
```

Each folder holds different types of static content, making it easier to manage and update.

Testing Static File Serving

To test that your static files are being served correctly:

- Place some test files in the appropriate directories within the **`static`** folder.
- Run your Go server.
- Open a web browser and go to **`http://localhost:8080/images/logo.png`** or whatever the path to your static file is.

If set up correctly, the browser should display the image or the content of the static file. For **`gitforgits.com`**, serving static files efficiently allows the website to load faster and gives the user a better experience. For example, when a user visits the website, the HTML content structured with corresponding CSS styles and interactive JavaScript can be served quickly from the server without needing to be processed dynamically.

Structuring Go Web Application

For a Go web app to remain scalable, manageable, and clear as it becomes more complex, proper organization and structure are of the utmost importance. A well-organized framework will make it easier to manage gitforgits.com's many moving parts, including routing, database interactions, and business logic. Throughout the book, we will follow this detailed approach to building a typical Go web application.

Project Structure Overview

A well-organized Go project typically divides its components into directories that reflect their functionality. Following is a recommended structure for **`gitforgits.com`**:

```
/gitforgits.com

 /cmd

 /server

 - main.go

 /internal

 /api

 - handlers.go
```

```
/model
- models.go
/store
- db.go
/pkg
/config
- config.go
/static
/css
- style.css
/js
- app.js
/images
- logo.png
/templates
- index.html
/configs
- config.yaml
/scripts
- setup.sh
/docs
```

```
- api.md
```

Directories Overview

- /cmd
  - This directory contains the main applications for the project. Each application has its own subdirectory, named for what it does. For **gitforgits.com**, **server** might be the only subdirectory here, containing **main.go** which is the entry point of the web server.
- /internal
  - Holds private application and library code. This is where the bulk of our code lives. The **internal** directory is not importable by other code outside the project root.
  - /api contains the route handlers that connect your incoming requests to the appropriate logic.
  - /model includes definitions of data structures and domain logic.
  - /store deals with database operations like queries and updates.
- /pkg
  - Intended for code that can be used by other applications (reusable code).
  - /config might handle loading configuration files.
- /static and /templates
  - **static** holds static files like CSS, JavaScript, and images.
  - **templates** contains your HTML templates which could be rendered and served by your handlers.
- /configs
  - Configuration files (like YAML, JSON, or TOML) that configure the application itself and other components like databases, are placed here.
- /scripts
  - Contains scripts for various build, install, analysis, etc. It's not for application scripts. For example, database migration scripts could be here.
- /docs
  - Documentation for the project. This could be API documentation, architecture

diagrams, etc.

Sample Program: Adopting Structure in gitforgits.com

Given below is how the application entry point and a handler might look following this structure:

- /cmd/server/main.go

```
package main

import (
 "net/http"
 "gitforgits.com/internal/api"
)

func main() {
 http.HandleFunc("/", api.HandleIndex)
 http.HandleFunc("/books", api.HandleBooks)
 http.ListenAndServe(":8080", nil)
}
```

- /internal/api/handlers.go

```
package api

import (
 "fmt"
 "net/http"
```

```
 "gitforgits.com/internal/model"
)

// HandleIndex serves the main page.
func HandleIndex(w http.ResponseWriter, r *http.Request)
{
 fmt.Fprintf(w, "Welcome to gitforgits.com!")
}

// HandleBooks displays books available.
func HandleBooks(w http.ResponseWriter, r *http.Request)
{
 books := model.FetchBooks() // Assume FetchBooks returns
a list of books
 for _, book := range books {
 fmt.Fprintf(w, "Book: %s\n", book.Title)
 }
}
```

- /internal/model/models.go

```
package model

// Book represents a book in the store.
```

```
type Book struct {
 Title string
 Author string
 Pages int
}

// FetchBooks simulates fetching books from a database.
func FetchBooks() []Book {
 return []Book{
 {Title: "The Go Programming Language", Author: "Alan A.
A. Donovan", Pages: 380},
 {Title: "Go in Action", Author: "William Kennedy",
Pages: 300},
 }
}
```

Such above structure lays out the puzzle pieces of any application in a way that new developers and system maintainers can easily follow, making it easier to comprehend how the system works and where specific features are put into play. The remaining chapters of this book will adhere consistently to this structure, making sure that the codebase for gitforgits.com is coherent and easy to maintain.

Summary

In this chapter, we looked at the practical aspects of creating a web server with Go's net/http package, which is essential for any web application. We began by learning the package's capabilities, particularly how it facilitates the creation and management of HTTP servers. We learned how to configure a simple HTTP server, including how to write server-side code that listens for and responds to HTTP requests. As a result, you were needed to be familiar with the many HTTP methods—GET, POST, PUT, DELETE, and more—that are essential to running RESTful services.

We tried routing using http.ServeMux which allowed us to route incoming requests to specific handler functions based on their URL path. For a well-organized and effective backend, where various tasks, such as retrieving book information or processing user data, are clearly separated, this is necessary.

The chapter also demonstrated how to dynamically respond to user requests using query parameters and URL fragments. These elements improve the server's ability to deliver content that responds to user input, such as filtering book lists or directing users to specific parts of a webpage, without requiring new requests from the server.

We also looked into serving static files and assets, which is critical for delivering JavaScript, CSS, and image files that make up the visual and interactive components of gitforgits.com. Finally, we organized our Go web application project's directory hierarchy, ensuring that it is scalable and maintainable. This configuration not only facilitates development but also simplifies future enhancements and debugging. Each of these components lays the groundwork for more complex functionalities in subsequent chapters, bringing us closer to a fully operational e-commerce platform for selling books.

CHAPTER 3: ADVANCED ROUTING WITH GORILLA/MUX

Chapter Overview

This chapter focuses on advanced web routing techniques with the **gorilla/mux** package, a powerful extension to Go's standard **net/http** library that was created specifically to improve the routing capabilities of web applications like **gitforgits.com**. This chapter will help you better understand more sophisticated routing options that provide more flexibility and control over request handling.

We begin with an introduction to **gorilla/mux**, exploring its advantages over the basic **http.ServeMux** and why it's a preferred choice for complex applications. The chapter will include how **gorilla/mux** supports methods that facilitate the development of scalable and maintainable web servers. Next, we look into advanced routing techniques, explaining how **gorilla/mux** allows for detailed routes that can include regular expressions and path variables. This capability enables developers to create more dynamic and variable-driven routes, crucial for applications requiring detailed parameter handling within URLs. We also explore custom handlers and middleware, important features for managing cross-cutting concerns such as logging, security, and session management across requests. Understanding middleware in **gorilla/mux** will help you build secure and well-logged applications, improving both reliability and maintainability.

Error handling and HTTP status codes are also covered in this chapter, providing strategies to handle errors gracefully and communicate effectively with clients about the state of their requests. This includes setting appropriate HTTP status codes and crafting error messages that assist in debugging and user guidance. The chapter progresses to implementing RESTful routing, demonstrating how to structure your application for RESTful architecture using **gorilla/mux**. This section is particularly valuable for building services that are easy to integrate with other services and clients, a typical requirement in modern web development.

Building CRUD operations is another critical aspect we address, detailing how to use **gorilla/mux** to handle create, read, update, and delete operations efficiently. This part is vital for **gitforgits.com** as it forms the backbone of managing book entries and user interactions on the platform. This comprehensive approach ensures that by the end of the chapter, you will be proficient in using **gorilla/mux** to build a robust, efficient, and secure web application for **gitforgits.com**.

Introduction to gorilla/mux

Gorilla Mux is a versatile and powerful URL router and dispatcher for Go that extends the capabilities of the standard **net/http ServeMux**. It is a key component of developing sophisticated web applications and is particularly well suited to scenarios requiring complex and nuanced routing decisions, such as our project, gitforgits.com. Knowing how Gorilla Mux improves upon **ServeMux** can help you design and build better backend services.

Why Gorilla Mux?

Gorilla Mux provides several advanced features that are not available with the standard **`http.ServeMux`**, making it a superior choice for web applications that require detailed and flexible routing capabilities:

- **Variable Path Segments**: Gorilla Mux supports variables in routing patterns, allowing dynamic segments within the URL path. This is particularly useful for REST APIs where you might have a URL like **`/books/{id}`** and need to capture the **`id`** part as a variable.
- **Regular Expression Routing**: It allows defining routes using regular expressions, which gives you more control over what URLs can match a route.
- **Method-Based Routing**: Unlike **`http.ServeMux`**, Gorilla Mux allows you to distinguish routes based on HTTP methods. This means you can have different handlers for GET, POST, PUT, etc., on the same URL pattern.
- **Subrouters**: Gorilla Mux supports the creation of subrouters, which are particularly useful for larger applications. Subrouters allow you to segment your routing into manageable pieces, each of which can have middleware or specific settings applied.
- **Custom Matchers**: You can write custom matchers to decide whether a route should match based on the request headers, query parameters, or any other properties of the request.
- **Clean and Precise URL Matching**: Gorilla Mux does not automatically redirect paths like the standard **`http.ServeMux`**. For example, if you register a route for **`/books`**, it will not automatically match **`/books/`**. This strict matching helps avoid unwanted behavior from misconfiguration and makes routes predictable.

Up and Running with Gorilla Mux

To begin using Gorilla Mux in our **`gitforgits.com`** project, we first need to install it. Gorilla Mux is not part of the standard library, so it requires an external package installation:

```
go get -u github.com/gorilla/mux
```

Once installed, you can start using it by importing it into your Go application. Following is a simple example that demonstrates creating a new router, registering some routes, and starting an HTTP server:

```
package main
```

```
import (
 "fmt"
 "net/http"
 "github.com/gorilla/mux"
)

func main() {
 r := mux.NewRouter()

 // Register routes using methods to handle different
types of requests
 r.HandleFunc("/books", getBooks).Methods("GET")
 r.HandleFunc("/books", createBook).Methods("POST")
 r.HandleFunc("/books/{id}", getBook).Methods("GET")

 http.ListenAndServe(":8080", r)
}

func getBooks(w http.ResponseWriter, r *http.Request) {
 fmt.Fprintln(w, "Retrieving all books")
}
```

```
func createBook(w http.ResponseWriter, r *http.Request) {
 fmt.Fprintln(w, "Creating a new book")
}

func getBook(w http.ResponseWriter, r *http.Request) {
 vars := mux.Vars(r)
 id := vars["id"]
 fmt.Fprintf(w, "Retrieving book with ID: %s", id)
}
```

In the above code snippet,

- We instantiate a Gorilla Mux router with **mux.NewRouter()**.
- We define multiple handlers for different HTTP methods at similar routes. This demonstrates how Gorilla Mux easily differentiates between different methods on the same path.
- We use path variables (**{id}**) to capture parts of the URL that can vary, like an ID.

As we advance in the book, Gorilla Mux will facilitate the development of a backend that is more organized and packed with functionalities, thereby catering to the complex requirements of a dynamic platform for book sales.

Advanced Routing Techniques

Gorilla Mux's advanced routing techniques make handling HTTP requests more flexible and functional. When it comes to managing complicated routing patterns, these techniques are beneficial for **gitforgits.com**. In this section, we shall look into three advanced routing techniques that add complexity to routing decisions: managing query parameters, handling subdomains, and using regular expressions for route patterns.

Regular Expression Constraints

Gorilla Mux allows the use of regular expressions to define constraints on variable routes, making it possible to match routes based on specific patterns. This can be invaluable when you need to ensure that a variable in a route meets certain criteria, such as a specific format or range.

Suppose you want to ensure that the book ID in the route is always a numeric value. You can define a route with a regular expression constraint to enforce this:

```
package main


import (
 "fmt"
 "net/http"
 "github.com/gorilla/mux"
)


func main() {
 r := mux.NewRouter()
 r.HandleFunc("/books/{id:[0-9]+}",
getBook).Methods("GET")


 http.ListenAndServe(":8080", r)
}


func getBook(w http.ResponseWriter, r *http.Request) {
 vars := mux.Vars(r)
 id := vars["id"]
```

```
 fmt.Fprintf(w, "Retrieving book with numeric ID: %s",
id)

}
```

In this setup, the **{id:[0-9]+}** in the route specifies that the **id** must be one or more digits. Requests with non-numeric **id** will not match this route.

Subdomain Routing

Subdomain routing can be crucial for applications like **gitforgits.com** that may have different subdomains for various functions, such as admin areas or user-specific sites. Gorilla Mux can handle routes based on the hostname, allowing you to direct traffic to different parts of your application depending on the subdomain.

For example, let us say we want to handle routes for an admin subdomain:

```
package main


import (

 "fmt"

 "net/http"

 "github.com/gorilla/mux"

)


func main() {

 r := mux.NewRouter()


 // Create a subrouter for the admin subdomain

 adminRouter :=
```

```
r.Host("admin.gitforgits.com").Subrouter()
 adminRouter.HandleFunc("/", adminIndex).Methods("GET")


 http.ListenAndServe(":8080", r)
}


func adminIndex(w http.ResponseWriter, r *http.Request) {
 fmt.Fprintln(w, "Admin dashboard")
}
```

In the above code snippet, **adminRouter** is configured to respond only to requests that target the **admin.gitforgits.com** hostname, directing users to an admin-specific part of the site.

Query Parameter Routing

While Gorilla Mux does not natively support routing based on query parameters directly in its route patterns, you can achieve this by using custom matchers or by handling the logic within your handlers to provide different responses based on query parameters.

For example, what if we wanted to customize a book listing page to display different genres depending on a query parameter:

```
package main


import (
 "fmt"
 "net/http"
 "github.com/gorilla/mux"
)
```

```
func main() {
 r := mux.NewRouter()
 r.HandleFunc("/books", listBooks).Methods("GET")

 http.ListenAndServe(":8080", r)
}

func listBooks(w http.ResponseWriter, r *http.Request) {
 genre := r.URL.Query().Get("genre")
 if genre != "" {
 fmt.Fprintf(w, "Listing books from genre: %s", genre)
 } else {
 fmt.Fprintln(w, "Listing all books")
 }
}
```

This code doesn't use Gorilla Mux's routing directly for the query parameter but instead, checks the **`genre`** query parameter within the handler and adjusts the response accordingly.

These three techniques—regular expression constraints, subdomain routing, and query parameter handling—provide robust tools for building complex routing logic in your web applications. They allow for precise control over how requests are handled, making your application more flexible and capable of addressing a variety of routing needs.

Path Variables

Path variables, sometimes called route parameters, make it possible to parameterize URLs, which means that given a set of variables in the URL's path, the same pattern of URLs can serve different data. Accessing user profiles, retrieving specific book details, or editing them can be made easier with the help of path variables on **gitforgits.com**. Now that we know how to define, identify, and access path variables using standard Go **net/http**, we dive into how to use Gorilla Mux, which enhances these capabilities even further.

Defining Path Variables

In Gorilla Mux, path variables are defined directly within the route pattern by enclosing them in curly braces **{}**. This tells the router that the section of the URL is variable and should be captured as a parameter.

Suppose we want to create a route that captures a book ID from the URL:

```
r.HandleFunc("/books/{id}", bookHandler)
```

In this pattern, **{id}** is a path variable that will match any string that occupies that position in the URL path. When a request is made, whatever value is in that position will be captured as the **id**.

Accessing Path Variables

Once a path variable is defined in a route, it can be accessed within the handler using the **Vars** function provided by Gorilla Mux. This function returns a map of the route variables for the current request, keyed by the variable name as defined in the route pattern. Let us say, we want to access the book ID in the handler:

```
func bookHandler(w http.ResponseWriter, r *http.Request)
{
 vars := mux.Vars(r)
 bookID := vars["id"]
 fmt.Fprintf(w, "Book ID: %s", bookID)
}
```

In the above script, **mux.Vars(r)** retrieves a map containing all path variables, and we access the **id** using the key **"id"**, which corresponds to our route definition. We will consider practical scenarios where path variables are beneficial for **gitforgits.com**:

- By using a path variable to specify the book ID in the URL, we can create a clean and intuitive API endpoint for retrieving book details.

```
r.HandleFunc("/books/{id}", getBook).Methods("GET")
```

- Similarly, path variables can be used to specify which book needs to be updated, using the same base URL but with a different HTTP method.

```
r.HandleFunc("/books/{id}", updateBook).Methods("PUT")
```

- Use a DELETE method with a path variable to specify the book to be removed.

```
r.HandleFunc("/books/{id}", deleteBook).Methods("DELETE")
```

Managing Path Variables

When working with path variables, it's important to validate and manage the incoming data. Since path variables are part of the URL, they are directly exposed to users and can be a vector for invalid data or security risks.

Following are a few considerations:

- Always validate path variables before using them in your application logic. For instance, if an ID should be numeric, validate that the received ID is indeed a number before querying the database.
- Provide clear error messages or responses when a path variable does not meet the expected format or does not correspond to a real resource in the application.

Let us consider an example of validating a numeric book ID and handling errors:

```
func getBook(w http.ResponseWriter, r *http.Request) {

 vars := mux.Vars(r)

 bookID := vars["id"]



 // Simulate ID validation

 if _, err := strconv.Atoi(bookID); err != nil {
```

```
http.Error(w, "Invalid book ID", http.StatusBadRequest)

return

}


fmt.Fprintf(w, "Fetching book with ID: %s", bookID)

}
```

In this snippet, we use **strconv.Atoi** to check if the **id** is a valid integer. If it's not, we send a **400 Bad Request** response. Web routing's path variables allow for dynamic and flexible URL patterns, which is a powerful feature. The development of RESTful APIs for the efficient management of gitforgits.com resources, such as books or user accounts, is made possible by them.

Regex-based Routing

One of the most useful features of Gorilla Mux and other modern web routing systems is regex-based routing, which lets programmers specify routes with greater precision and granularity by means of regular expressions. Because they allow for the specification of patterns in strings, regular expressions (regex) are perfect for matching complicated route structures in a web application.

Understanding Regex

Regular expressions are patterns used to match sequences of characters in strings. In the context of web routing, they can be used to enforce specific formats for path variables or to differentiate routes based on complex rules that go beyond simple path matching.

For example, a regular expression **^[0-9]+$** matches a sequence of one or more numeric characters. This can be particularly useful in routes where numeric identifiers such as user IDs, book IDs, or other parameters need strict validation.

Advantages of Regex-Based Routing

Regex-based routing offers several advantages over standard routing:

- Regex allows routes to be defined with exact character-level control, reducing the chance of incorrect matches.

- It can validate the format of path segments directly within the route definition, ensuring that only correctly formatted requests are routed to the handler.
- Regex routes can handle a wide variety of URL structures without needing multiple similar route entries, keeping the routing table cleaner and more manageable.

Implementing Regex-Based Routing

Gorilla Mux supports regex-based routing directly in the route definitions by allowing you to specify regular expressions for path variables. We will see how to apply this in a practical example for **gitforgits.com**.

Suppose we want to ensure that the book ID in the URL is a numeric string of exactly 5 digits. We can define a route in Gorilla Mux using a regular expression to enforce this:

```
package main


import (
 "fmt"
 "net/http"
 "github.com/gorilla/mux"
)


func main() {
 r := mux.NewRouter()


 // Define a route with a regex constraint
 r.HandleFunc("/books/{id:[0-9]{5}}",
getBook).Methods("GET")
```

```
 http.ListenAndServe(":8080", r)
}

func getBook(w http.ResponseWriter, r *http.Request) {
 vars := mux.Vars(r)
 bookID := vars["id"]
 fmt.Fprintf(w, "Fetching book with ID: %s", bookID)
}
```

In the above sample program,

- The route **"/books/{id:[0-9]{5}}"** includes a regex pattern **[0-9]{5}** which specifies that the **id** must consist of exactly 5 digits.
- This ensures that only URLs with a five-digit book ID will match this route; all other requests will not trigger the **getBook** handler.

Testing Regex-Based Routing

To test this route, you could use a tool like **curl** or visit the URL in a browser:

- A request to **http://localhost:8080/books/12345** should successfully reach the **getBook** handler and return the corresponding book ID.
- A request to **http://localhost:8080/books/123** or **http://localhost:8080/books/abcde** would fail to match the route, resulting in a 404 Not Found error, as these do not meet the regex criteria.

It safeguards **gitforgits.com** by processing only correctly formatted requests, which can lessen the likelihood of mistakes and increase safety. A dynamic, data-driven website has specific requirements, and Gorilla Mux's usage of regular expressions allows it to efficiently handle complex routing needs.

Custom Handlers and Middleware

When building strong web apps, custom handlers and middleware are must-haves. They let you efficiently process HTTP requests and do actions on a global scale with each request. If we ever have to systematically deal with authentication, logging, and request validation across various portions of gitforgits.com, this will be a lifesaver.

Purpose of Custom Handlers and Middleware

Custom Handlers are specialized functions or objects that handle HTTP requests. They are designed to execute specific tasks, such as responding to particular endpoints or performing operations like rendering a web page or returning JSON data.

Middleware is a piece of software that hooks into the request/response lifecycle. It acts on the requests before they reach the actual handlers and/or after the handlers have processed the requests. Middleware can be used for logging, authentication, CORS (Cross-Origin Resource Sharing), caching, etc.

They are incredibly useful for:

- Enforcing security measures, like checking authentication tokens.
- Modifying request or response objects, like setting common headers or compressing responses.
- Logging or monitoring the requests and responses.

Creating Custom Handlers and Middleware in Gorilla Mux

In Gorilla Mux, both custom handlers and middleware can be easily implemented and integrated into the routing system.

Custom Handlers

A custom handler is typically created by implementing the **`http.Handler`** interface, which requires a method **`ServeHTTP(w http.ResponseWriter, r *http.Request)`**.

Following is a simple custom handler for **`gitforgits.com`**:

```
type BookHandler struct {

 message string

}


func (h *BookHandler) ServeHTTP(w http.ResponseWriter, r
*http.Request) {
```

```
 fmt.Fprintf(w, h.message)
}
```

This **BookHandler** is a custom handler that writes a message stored in the handler to the response.

Middleware

Middleware in Gorilla Mux can be implemented as functions that take an **http.Handler** and return a new **http.Handler**. This allows them to execute code before and after the handler is called.

Following is an example of a logging middleware:

```
func LoggingMiddleware(next http.Handler) http.Handler {
 return http.HandlerFunc(func(w http.ResponseWriter, r
*http.Request) {
 log.Printf("Request received: %s %s", r.Method,
r.URL.Path)
 next.ServeHTTP(w, r)
 log.Printf("Request handled successfully")
 })
}
```

This middleware logs each request when it's received and after it's handled.

Sample Program: Manage Routing with Custom Handlers

We shall now integrate the above learned concepts into the **gitforgits.com** project by setting up a router with custom handlers and middleware:

```
package main
```

```
import (
 "fmt"
 "log"
 "net/http"
 "github.com/gorilla/mux"
)

func main() {
 r := mux.NewRouter()

 // Middleware setup
 r.Use(LoggingMiddleware)

 // Setting up the custom handler
 bookHandler := &BookHandler{message: "Welcome to
GitforGits Books!"}
 r.Handle("/books", bookHandler)

 http.ListenAndServe(":8080", r)
}

// BookHandler is a custom HTTP handler for serving book
```

```
requests.
type BookHandler struct {
 message string
}

func (h *BookHandler) ServeHTTP(w http.ResponseWriter, r
*http.Request) {
 fmt.Fprintf(w, h.message)
}

// LoggingMiddleware logs each HTTP request.
func LoggingMiddleware(next http.Handler) http.Handler {
 return http.HandlerFunc(func(w http.ResponseWriter, r
*http.Request) {
 log.Printf("Request received: %s %s", r.Method,
r.URL.Path)
 next.ServeHTTP(w, r)
 log.Printf("Request handled successfully")
 })
}
```

In this setup, **gitforgits.com** uses custom handlers to manage specific routing paths while employing middleware for logging across all requests. This structure not only enhances the modularity and maintainability of the application but also ensures that essential operations like logging and security are consistently applied.

Error Handling and HTTP Status Codes

The development of robust and user-friendly web applications relies heavily on the correct usage of HTTP status codes and efficient error handling. When something goes wrong on gitforgits.com, users get clear feedback from the robust error handling system, which helps with troubleshooting and improves the user experience overall.

Understanding HTTP Status Codes

HTTP status codes are standardized codes in HTTP responses that indicate the result of the attempted understanding or satisfying of the request. They are grouped into several categories:

- **1xx (Informational)**: Communicate transfer protocol-level information.
- **2xx (Success)**: Indicate that the client's request was accepted successfully.
- **3xx (Redirection)**: Indicate that further actions need to be taken by the client in order to complete the request.
- **4xx (Client Error)**: Indicate errors made by the client, such as a bad request or unauthorized access.
- **5xx (Server Error)**: Indicate problems on the server-side which prevent it from fulfilling a valid request.

Implementing Error Handling

When working with Go, especially with Gorilla Mux, middleware, custom error responses, and logging make it easy to handle errors and respond with the right HTTP status codes.

First, we will take a look at these mechanisms and see how they work.

Custom Error Handler

Creating a custom error handler function can help encapsulate the error handling logic, making your application cleaner and more organized. Given below is an example of a simple error handler that logs the error and sends an appropriate HTTP response:

```
func ErrorHandler(w http.ResponseWriter, r *http.Request,
status int, err error) {

 log.Printf("HTTP %d - %s", status, err)

 http.Error(w, http.StatusText(status), status)
```

```
}
```

This function logs the error and uses **http.Error** to send a response with the correct status code and message.

Using Middleware for Error Handling

Middleware can be used to catch errors and handle them gracefully. Given below is an example of a middleware function that intercepts the response before it's sent to the client:

```
func ErrorHandlingMiddleware(next http.Handler)
http.Handler {

 return http.HandlerFunc(func(w http.ResponseWriter, r
*http.Request) {

 defer func() {

 if err := recover(); err != nil {

 log.Println("Recovered from error:", err)

 ErrorHandler(w, r, http.StatusInternalServerError,
fmt.Errorf("internal server error"))

 }

 }()

 next.ServeHTTP(w, r)

 })

}
```

This middleware uses **recover** to catch any panics in the application, logging the error, and sending a generic 500 Internal Server Error to keep the application from crashing and to avoid exposing sensitive error details.

Sample Program: Handling Specific Errors

Consider handling a common error scenario like a "not found" error in the book resource.

Following is how you might implement it:

```
func getBookHandler(w http.ResponseWriter, r
*http.Request) {
 vars := mux.Vars(r)
 bookID := vars["id"]
 book, err := fetchBookByID(bookID)
 if err != nil {
 if err == ErrBookNotFound {
 ErrorHandler(w, r, http.StatusNotFound, err)
 return
 }
 ErrorHandler(w, r, http.StatusInternalServerError, err)
 return
 }
 fmt.Fprintf(w, "Book found: %+v", book)
}

// Simulate a function to fetch a book by ID
func fetchBookByID(id string) (*Book, error) {
 // Example: Book not found
 return nil, ErrBookNotFound
}
```

```
var ErrBookNotFound = errors.New("book not found")
```

In this handler, **fetchBookByID** simulates fetching a book by its ID. If the book is not found, it returns an **ErrBookNotFound** error, which the handler checks and responds to with a 404 Not Found status. For other errors, it responds with a 500 Internal Server Error. By implementing structured error handling using custom handlers and middleware, gitforgits.com can provide clear, useful feedback to the user and maintain stability by managing server-side errors effectively.

Perform RESTful Routing

Web services built using the REST (Representational State Transfer) architectural style rely heavily on RESTful routing to execute CRUD (Create, Read, Update, Delete) operations using standard HTTP methods. In the context of our project, **gitforgits.com**, implementing RESTful routing ensures that the web services are both intuitive and scalable, facilitating easy interaction between the client-side and server-side components.

Understanding RESTful Routing

RESTful routing uses standard HTTP methods to correspond to basic database operations:

- **GET**: Retrieve data from the server (Read operation).
- **POST**: Submit new data to the server (Create operation).
- **PUT**: Update existing data on the server (Update operation).
- **DELETE**: Remove existing data from the server (Delete operation).

Each resource, such as a user or a book on **gitforgits.com**, typically has a specific URI (Uniform Resource Identifier) and can be interacted with using these HTTP methods.

Implementing RESTful Routing using Gorilla Mux

To implement RESTful routing in our project, we will use Gorilla Mux, which provides enhanced capabilities for route handling that go beyond the standard **net/http** library.

We will set up a simple RESTful API for the book resource.

Setting up Gorilla Mux Router

First, we need to set up the Gorilla Mux router in our main application file:

```
package main
```

```
import (
 "net/http"
 "github.com/gorilla/mux"
)

func main() {
 r := mux.NewRouter()
 r.HandleFunc("/books", getBooks).Methods("GET")
 r.HandleFunc("/books", createBook).Methods("POST")
 r.HandleFunc("/books/{id}", getBook).Methods("GET")
 r.HandleFunc("/books/{id}", updateBook).Methods("PUT")
 r.HandleFunc("/books/{id}",
deleteBook).Methods("DELETE")

 http.ListenAndServe(":8080", r)
}
```

Defining Handler Functions

Each route handler will perform actions corresponding to the REST operations.

Fetching all books:

```
func getBooks(w http.ResponseWriter, r *http.Request) {
 // Logic to fetch all books
```

```
 fmt.Fprintln(w, "Fetching all books")
}
```

Creating a new book:

```
func createBook(w http.ResponseWriter, r *http.Request) {
 // Logic to create a new book
 fmt.Fprintln(w, "Creating new book")
}
```

Fetching a specific book by ID:

```
func getBook(w http.ResponseWriter, r *http.Request) {
 vars := mux.Vars(r)
 bookID := vars["id"]
 // Logic to fetch a specific book using bookID
 fmt.Fprintf(w, "Fetching book with ID: %s", bookID)
}
```

Updating a specific book:

```
func updateBook(w http.ResponseWriter, r *http.Request) {
 vars := mux.Vars(r)
 bookID := vars["id"]
 // Logic to update a book using bookID
 fmt.Fprintf(w, "Updating book with ID: %s", bookID)
}
```

Deleting a specific book:

```
func deleteBook(w http.ResponseWriter, r *http.Request) {
 vars := mux.Vars(r)
 bookID := vars["id"]
 // Logic to delete a book using bookID
 fmt.Fprintf(w, "Deleting book with ID: %s", bookID)
}
```

In **gitforgits.com**, these RESTful routes allow clients to interact with the book data in a standardized way. For example, a mobile app or a web frontend can easily understand how to make requests to add, fetch, update, or delete books using standard HTTP methods. This consistency across different platforms and technologies ensures that **gitforgits.com** can be easily integrated with other services and tools.

Building CRUD Operations

Creating a CRUD (Create, Read, Update, Delete) API is essential for managing data dynamically as such a CRUD API will allow us to handle book data effectively, facilitating operations such as adding new books, retrieving book details, updating existing books, and deleting books.

Given below is how we can build a CRUD API using Go and Gorilla Mux, leveraging what we've learned about RESTful routing and applying it to perform these fundamental database operations.

Setting up the Environment

First, ensure you have Gorilla Mux installed, as it will handle our HTTP routing:

```
go get -u github.com/gorilla/mux
```

Defining Book Model

Before we create the handlers for our CRUD operations, we define a simple model for our **Book** entity. This model will be used to simulate a database of books.

```
package main
```

```
import "errors"

var books = []*Book{
 {ID: "1", Title: "1984", Author: "George Orwell"},
 {ID: "2", Title: "The Great Gatsby", Author: "F. Scott
Fitzgerald"},
}

type Book struct {
 ID string
 Title string
 Author string
}

func findBookByID(id string) (*Book, error) {
 for _, book := range books {
 if book.ID == id {
 return book, nil
 }
 }
 return nil, errors.New("book not found")
```

```
}

func addBook(book *Book) {
 books = append(books, book)
}

func updateBook(id string, updated *Book) error {
 for i, book := range books {
 if book.ID == id {
 books[i] = updated
 return nil
 }
 }
 return errors.New("book not found")
}

func deleteBook(id string) error {
 for i, book := range books {
 if book.ID == id {
 books = append(books[:i], books[i+1:]...)
 return nil
```

```
 }
 }
 return errors.New("book not found")
}
```

Building Handlers

With the model in place, we can now create handlers for each CRUD operation.

Create (POST)

```
func createBookHandler(w http.ResponseWriter, r
*http.Request) {
 var book Book
 if err := json.NewDecoder(r.Body).Decode(&book); err !=
nil {
 http.Error(w, err.Error(), http.StatusBadRequest)
 return
 }
 addBook(&book)
 w.WriteHeader(http.StatusCreated)
 json.NewEncoder(w).Encode(book)
}
```

Read (GET)

```
func getBooksHandler(w http.ResponseWriter, r
*http.Request) {
```

```
json.NewEncoder(w).Encode(books)
}


func getBookHandler(w http.ResponseWriter, r
*http.Request) {
 vars := mux.Vars(r)
 book, err := findBookByID(vars["id"])
 if err != nil {
 http.Error(w, err.Error(), http.StatusNotFound)
 return
 }
 json.NewEncoder(w).Encode(book)
}
```

Update (PUT)

```
func updateBookHandler(w http.ResponseWriter, r
*http.Request) {
 vars := mux.Vars(r)
 id := vars["id"]
 var updatedBook Book
 if err := json.NewDecoder(r.Body).Decode(&updatedBook);
err != nil {
 http.Error(w, err.Error(), http.StatusBadRequest)
```

```
 return
 }
 if err := updateBook(id, &updatedBook); err != nil {
 http.Error(w, err.Error(), http.StatusNotFound)
 return
 }
 json.NewEncoder(w).Encode(updatedBook)
}
```

Delete (DELETE)

```
func deleteBookHandler(w http.ResponseWriter, r
*http.Request) {
 vars := mux.Vars(r)
 if err := deleteBook(vars["id"]); err != nil {
 http.Error(w, err.Error(), http.StatusNotFound)
 return
 }
 w.WriteHeader(http.StatusNoContent)
}
```

Assembling the Router and Starting the Server

Now that all handlers are defined, we set up the routing and start the server.

```
func main() {
```

```
r := mux.NewRouter()

r.HandleFunc("/books", getBooksHandler).Methods("GET")

r.HandleFunc("/books",
createBookHandler).Methods("POST")

r.HandleFunc("/books/{id}",
getBookHandler).Methods("GET")

r.HandleFunc("/books/{id}",
updateBookHandler).Methods("PUT")

r.HandleFunc("/books/{id}",
deleteBookHandler).Methods("DELETE")

http.ListenAndServe(":8080", r)

}
```

The above configuration of gitforgits.com generates a fully functional CRUD API for book management. You can access all parts of the CRUD operation using standard HTTP methods, so the application can manage book data efficiently.

Summary

This chapter explored advanced routing techniques with Gorilla Mux, which improved our ability to handle HTTP requests for gitforgits.com. As a first step, we learned Gorilla Mux that offers features such as method-specific routing, regex-based path matching, and support for path variables and subdomains.

We perfected the art of regex-based routing, which gives us complete command over the URL patterns to which our app can react. In addition, we touched on subdomain routing, which allows the application to provide different content or features depending on the hostname of the request. In order to keep sensitive information private, like administrative interfaces, this is a great feature to have on a website.

We learned to extract dynamic content from URLs, which is useful for retrieving specific data like a book ID, in the section on working with path variables. With this feature added to our server, we can now provide endpoints that are more interactive and flexible. Also covered were middleware and custom handlers, two of the most important tools for writing well-structured, reusable code. It was shown that middleware is a strong feature for managing cross-cutting concerns like request-level security and logging, which makes application development and maintenance easier.

Lastly, the chapter covered all the bases for creating a RESTful API with a CRUD interface using Gorilla Mux. To demonstrate how to apply these operations in a practical setting, we established routes to add, edit, and remove book entries. In addition to providing the foundation for managing book data, this CRUD implementation shows how the routing techniques covered in the chapter can be applied in practice.

CHAPTER 4: USER AUTHENTICATION WITH OAUTH2 AND JWT

Chapter Overview

In this chapter, we will take a deep dive into user authentication, a crucial area for gitforgits.com, and how to set up safe and effective systems to handle user identities and permissions. This chapter delves into the fundamental ideas and advanced methods of user authentication, resource protection, and making sure that the web platform is both secure and easy to use.

We begin with a brief overview of user authentication, learning its significance and outlining its operation in web applications. Next, we explore OAuth2, a popular authorization framework that lets apps get restricted access to HTTP service user accounts. To enable secure delegated access, we will learn how to apply OAuth2 in Go.

In addition, the chapter delves into the integration of popular ways to streamline the registration and login processes—like Google and Facebook—through their respective login systems. Importantly, we will also cover how to implement JSON Web Tokens (JWT) for API security. We will explore how to utilize JWTs to keep sessions secure across requests without requiring server-side session storage, and how they offer a robust method of securely transmitting information between parties as a JSON object.

Also covered is session and cookie management, which focuses on the safe handling of user sessions in an online application. This involves setting up and controlling cookies, which are essential for securely managing session data and keeping state. It also delves into user registration and password management, offering valuable insights into building secure systems for user data management. This includes topics such as hashing and securing passwords, as well as handling flows for password resets. Rate limiting and abuse prevention are the last topics covered. In order to keep gitforgits.com secure and usable, we will go over ways to stop brute force attacks and other abusive behaviors.

Basics of User Authentication

A key part of web application security is user authentication, which limits access to data and features to authorized users only. It's a system put in place to make sure the people attempting to access a website or network are who they say they are. This authentication process grants users access to resources according to their claimed identities and guarantees that they are who they say they are.

What is User Authentication?

At its core, user authentication is about validating credentials provided by a user against some form of stored data that confirms the user's identity. This could be anything from a simple username and password pair to more complex systems involving multi-factor authentication using biometrics, security tokens, or OTPs (One-Time Passwords).

Working of User Authentication

The process typically involves several key steps:

1. **Credential Submission**: The user provides credentials, commonly in the form of a username and password, via a client application interface.
2. **Credential Verification**: The server compares the provided credentials against the stored credentials. If the credentials match, access is granted.
3. **Session Creation**: Upon successful authentication, the server creates a session for the user and issues a token (like a session cookie or JWT), which the client must store and send with subsequent requests to access protected resources.
4. **Session Management**: The server tracks and manages user sessions, often using tokens that contain encoded information about the user's session state.

Following is the detailed breakdown of the user authentication process:

Credential Verification

When a user enters their username and password, these details are sent to the server, usually over a secure HTTPS connection to prevent eavesdropping. On the server side, the password is typically not stored in plain text for security reasons. Instead, it's stored in a hashed form using a hashing algorithm (e.g., bcrypt, SHA-256).

Following is a simple example of how a password might be verified:

```
import (
 "golang.org/x/crypto/bcrypt"
)


func verifyPassword(userPassword string, storedHash string) bool {
 err := bcrypt.CompareHashAndPassword([]byte(storedHash), []byte(userPassword))
 return err == nil
}
```

In this function, **bcrypt.CompareHashAndPassword** checks whether the user-provided password, when hashed, matches the stored hash.

Session Creation and Management

Upon verifying the user's credentials, the server creates a session. This session can be tracked using a session ID stored in a cookie or a token-based system like JWT.

Following is an example of how a session token might be created using JWT:

```
import (
 "github.com/dgrijalva/jwt-go"
 "time"
)

func createToken(userID string) (string, error) {
 token := jwt.New(jwt.SigningMethodHS256)

 // Claims
 claims := token.Claims.(jwt.MapClaims)
 claims["authorized"] = true
 claims["user_id"] = userID
 claims["exp"] = time.Now().Add(time.Hour * 24).Unix()

 // Generating token
 tokenString, err := token.SignedString(mySigningKey)
 if err != nil {
```

```
return "", err

}

return tokenString, nil

}
```

In this code snippet, a new JWT is created with an expiration time and includes the user ID as a claim. It is then signed with a secret key.

Using Authentication to Protect Routes

Once a user is authenticated, the token they receive must be sent with each request to access protected routes. Following is a simple example of a middleware that checks the validity of a token:

```
func isAuthenticated(next http.Handler) http.Handler {

return http.HandlerFunc(func(w http.ResponseWriter, r *http.Request) {

if r.Header.Get("Authorization") != "" {

// Validate token

next.ServeHTTP(w, r)

} else {

http.Error(w, "Forbidden", http.StatusForbidden)

}

})

}
```

This middleware function intercepts incoming requests and checks for a valid **Authorization** header. If it exists (and is valid, with additional logic not shown here for brevity), the request is allowed to proceed; otherwise, a 403 Forbidden status is returned.

By incorporating strong user authentication into gitforgits.com, could efficiently manage user preferences, access controls, and transactions, resulting in a trustworthy and secure online platform.

Using OAuth2 with Go

One powerful authorization framework is OAuth 2.0, which lets apps get limited access to user accounts on HTTP services like Google, Facebook, or Microsoft. By integrating OAuth2 into our app, users can log in with their existing social media accounts, which streamlines the login process and may lead to higher engagement and retention rates. This improves the user experience overall.

Setting up OAuth2

To implement OAuth2, we will use the popular library **golang.org/x/oauth2**, which provides robust support for integrating OAuth2 into Go applications. This setup involves several steps: registering the application with a provider (such as Google or Facebook), setting up the OAuth2 client, and handling the OAuth2 flows to authenticate users.

Register the Application

First, you need to register your application with an OAuth2 provider. For the below example, we choose Google:

1. Go to the Google Developers Console: https://console.developers.google.com/
2. Create a new project.
3. Under "Credentials", create new OAuth client ID credentials.
    - Select the application type, typically "Web application".
    - Set the authorized redirect URIs to your server's redirect endpoint (e.g., **http://localhost:8080/oauth2/callback**).

After registering, you will receive a client ID and client secret. These are used in your Go application to configure the OAuth2 client.

Setting up OAuth2 Client

- Install the OAuth2 Go package if you haven't already:

```
go get golang.org/x/oauth2
```

- Create a new Go file to configure the OAuth2 client with the credentials provided by the

OAuth provider:

```
package main

import (
 "golang.org/x/oauth2"
 "golang.org/x/oauth2/google"
 "net/http"
 "fmt"
)

var (
 googleOauthConfig = &oauth2.Config{
 RedirectURL: "http://localhost:8080/oauth2/callback",
 ClientID: "YOUR_CLIENT_ID", // Replace with your client
ID
 ClientSecret: "YOUR_CLIENT_SECRET", // Replace with your
client secret
 Scopes:
[]string{"https://www.googleapis.com/auth/userinfo.email"
},
 Endpoint: google.Endpoint,
 }
 // Some random string, typically generated per session
```

```
 oauthStateString = "pseudo-random"
)

func main() {
 http.HandleFunc("/", handleMain)
 http.HandleFunc("/login", handleGoogleLogin)
 http.HandleFunc("/oauth2/callback",
handleGoogleCallback)
 fmt.Println("Started running on http://localhost:8080")
 http.ListenAndServe(":8080", nil)
}

func handleMain(w http.ResponseWriter, r *http.Request) {
 fmt.Fprintln(w, "Hello, world!")
}

func handleGoogleLogin(w http.ResponseWriter, r
*http.Request) {
 url := googleOauthConfig.AuthCodeURL(oauthStateString,
oauth2.AccessTypeOffline)
 http.Redirect(w, r, url, http.StatusTemporaryRedirect)
}
```

```
func handleGoogleCallback(w http.ResponseWriter, r
*http.Request) {

 // Handle the exchange code to initiate a transport.

 if r.URL.Query().Get("state") != oauthStateString {

 http.Error(w, "state did not match",
http.StatusBadRequest)

 return

 }


 token, err :=
googleOauthConfig.Exchange(oauth2.NoContext,
r.URL.Query().Get("code"))

 if err != nil {

 http.Error(w, "Failed to exchange token: "+err.Error(),
http.StatusInternalServerError)

 return

 }


 fmt.Fprintf(w, "Content: %+v", token)

}
```

In the above code:

- **googleOauthConfig** is configured with your client details and the scopes your application needs. The scopes determine what information you are requesting permission to access.

- **handleGoogleLogin** redirects the user to the Google login page.
- **handleGoogleCallback** handles the OAuth2 callback and token exchange.

Flows in OAuth2

The OAuth2 framework specifies several "flows" for different types of applications. The most common flow for web applications is the Authorization Code Grant, which is demonstrated in the above example.

This flow involves:

- Redirecting a user to the provider's authentication page.
- User authenticates and authorizes the application.
- User is redirected back to the application with an authorization code.
- The application exchanges the authorization code for an access token.

Not only does this configuration simplify authentication, but it also improves the user experience by letting users log in with their existing social media accounts.

Integration with Social Media Logins

Users' existing Facebook and Google accounts can also be utilized to streamline the authentication and registration process when social media logins are integrated into a web application. In particular, for our gitforgits.com, letting users log in through these services can improve the user experience by giving them a safer and faster alternative rather than creating and remembering a new set of credentials.

Integration with Google Login

We already set up the basic OAuth2 configuration for Google in our previous example. After the user is authenticated and you receive the OAuth token, you typically want to fetch user data from Google to create a user session.

Given below is how to modify the **handleGoogleCallback** function to fetch user details:

```
import (
 "encoding/json"
 "golang.org/x/oauth2"
```

```
"io/ioutil"
"net/http"
)

// This would be part of the googleOauthConfig setup
var googleOauthConfig = &oauth2.Config{
 // previous configuration...
}

func handleGoogleCallback(w http.ResponseWriter, r
*http.Request) {
 content, err :=
getUserDataFromGoogle(r.FormValue("code"))
 if err != nil {
 http.Error(w, err.Error(),
http.StatusInternalServerError)
 return
 }
 fmt.Fprintf(w, "User Info: %s", content)
}

func getUserDataFromGoogle(code string) (string, error) {
```

```
// Exchange the code for a token
token, err :=
googleOauthConfig.Exchange(oauth2.NoContext, code)
if err != nil {
return "", err
}

// Create a client to use the token
client := googleOauthConfig.Client(oauth2.NoContext,
token)
response, err :=
client.Get("https://www.googleapis.com/oauth2/v2/userinfo
")
if err != nil {
return "", err
}
defer response.Body.Close()
data, err := ioutil.ReadAll(response.Body)
if err != nil {
return "", err
}

return string(data), nil
```

```
}
```

In this code snippet, after exchanging the code for a token, we use the token to create an authenticated client. This client is then used to make a request to Google's user info endpoint, which returns details like the user's email, name, and profile picture.

Integration with Facebook Login

Integrating Facebook login involves steps similar to those for Google. First, you need to set up an application in the Facebook developer console, get your app credentials, and configure the OAuth2 setup in your Go application.

Setting up Facebook OAuth Configuration

```
var facebookOauthConfig = &oauth2.Config{
 RedirectURL:
"http://localhost:8080/oauth2/facebook/callback",
 ClientID: "YOUR_FACEBOOK_CLIENT_ID",
 ClientSecret: "YOUR_FACEBOOK_CLIENT_SECRET",
 Scopes: []string{"email"},
 Endpoint: oauth2.Endpoint{
 AuthURL: "https://www.facebook.com/v2.8/dialog/oauth",
 TokenURL:
"https://graph.facebook.com/v2.8/oauth/access_token",
 },
}
```

Handling Facebook Callback

The callback handler for Facebook would look quite similar to the Google one, but you would fetch user data from Facebook's graph API:

```
func handleFacebookCallback(w http.ResponseWriter, r
```

```
*http.Request) {
 content, err :=
getUserDataFromFacebook(r.FormValue("code"))
 if err != nil {
 http.Error(w, err.Error(),
http.StatusInternalServerError)
 return
 }
 fmt.Fprintf(w, "User Info: %s", content)
}

func getUserDataFromFacebook(code string) (string, error)
{
 token, err :=
facebookOauthConfig.Exchange(oauth2.NoContext, code)
 if err != nil {
 return "", err
 }

 // Fetch user data from Facebook's graph API
 client := facebookOauthConfig.Client(oauth2.NoContext,
token)
 response, err :=
client.Get("https://graph.facebook.com/me?fields=id,name,
```

```
email")
 if err != nil {
 return "", err
 }
 defer response.Body.Close()
 data, err := ioutil.ReadAll(response.Body)
 if err != nil {
 return "", err
 }

 return string(data), nil
}
```

Integration with Email Login

While social logins are convenient, providing an option for users to register and log in using their email address is also essential. This involves setting up a traditional registration and login form where users can enter their email and password. You would typically have an HTML form for registration and login that posts to your Go server. On the server side, you handle these posts, create new user records for registrations, and validate credentials for logins.

```
func handleRegistration(w http.ResponseWriter, r
*http.Request) {
 // Extract user details from r.FormValue("email"),
r.FormValue("password")
 // Create user logic here
 fmt.Fprintln(w, "Registration successful")
```

```
}

func handleLogin(w http.ResponseWriter, r *http.Request)
{
 // Validate login credentials
 // Authenticate session
 fmt.Fprintln(w, "Login successful")
}
```

Apps can provide users with more login options by combining OAuth2 with social media and supporting traditional email login methods. This gives users more control over their experience on the site and makes logging in easier, both of which improve the user experience.

Implementing JWT for Secure APIs

JSON Web Tokens (JWTs) are an open standard (RFC 7519) that define a compact and self-contained way for securely transmitting information between parties as a JSON object. This information can be verified and trusted because it is digitally signed. JWTs can be signed using a secret (with the HMAC algorithm) or a public/private key pair using RSA or ECDSA.

Advantages of JWT for Secure APIs

- **Compactness**: JWTs are compact, making them easy to transmit via URL, POST parameter, or inside an HTTP header.
- **Self-contained**: A JWT contains all the required information about the user, avoiding the need to query the database more than once.
- **Security**: The token is encrypted, providing security between two parties; a server can verify the token's authenticity to ensure that the token sender is who it says it is.
- **Cross-domain/Platform**: JWTs are useful across different domains and platforms, enhancing the flexibility in communication between disparate systems.
- **Performance**: Using JWT for session information reduces the need for server-side storage of session data, which can be particularly beneficial for scaling applications.

Implementing JWT

To implement JWTs, we will use the Go package **github.com/dgrijalva/jwt-go**, which provides the necessary tools to create and verify JWTs.

Install the JWT Go Package

First, install the JWT package:

```
go get -u github.com/dgrijalva/jwt-go
```

Create the JWT Token

We need a function to generate a JWT token after a user logs in. Given below is how you might implement this:

```
package main


import (
 "fmt"
 "time"
 "net/http"
 "github.com/dgrijalva/jwt-go"
)


var mySigningKey = []byte("secret") // Ensure to keep
this key safe


func GenerateJWT() (string, error) {
 token := jwt.New(jwt.SigningMethodHS256)
```

```
 claims := token.Claims.(jwt.MapClaims)


 claims["authorized"] = true

 claims["user_id"] = "123456"

 claims["exp"] = time.Now().Add(time.Hour * 24).Unix() //
Token expires after 24 hours


 tokenString, err := token.SignedString(mySigningKey)

 if err != nil {

 fmt.Errorf("Something Went Wrong: %s", err.Error())

 return "", err

 }


 return tokenString, nil

}
```

In this code, we create a new token that signs with the HMAC SHA256 algorithm. We include claims like user identification and expiry.

Setup HTTP Endpoint to use JWT

Create an endpoint that issues a token when hit:

```
func homePage(w http.ResponseWriter, r *http.Request) {

 validToken, err := GenerateJWT()

 if err != nil {
```

```
fmt.Fprintf(w, err.Error())
}
fmt.Fprintf(w, validToken)
}


func handleRequests() {
http.HandleFunc("/", homePage)
http.ListenAndServe(":9001", nil)
}
```

Create Middleware to Protect Routes

To utilize JWT for protecting certain routes, you can create middleware that checks for a valid token in the request headers:

```
func isAuthorized(endpoint func(http.ResponseWriter,
*http.Request)) http.Handler {
return http.HandlerFunc(func(w http.ResponseWriter, r
*http.Request) {


if r.Header["Token"] != nil {
token, err := jwt.Parse(r.Header["Token"][0], func(token
*jwt.Token) (interface{}, error) {
if _, ok := token.Method.(*jwt.SigningMethodHMAC); !ok {
return nil, fmt.Errorf("There was an error")
}
```

```
 return mySigningKey, nil
 })


 if err != nil {
 fmt.Fprintf(w, err.Error())
 }


 if token.Valid {
 endpoint(w, r)
 }
 } else {
 fmt.Fprintf(w, "Not Authorized")
 }
 })
}


func handleRequests() {
 http.Handle("/", isAuthorized(homePage))
 http.ListenAndServe(":9001", nil)
}
```

This middleware checks for a "Token" header and verifies it. If the token is valid, it calls the original endpoint; if not, it returns a "Not Authorized" response.

All in all, this configuration keeps user access rights tightly under control, improves the application's security and performance, and makes cross-platform interactions easier. In addition to protecting the app, this system offers a scalable way to authenticate users and manage their sessions.

Sessions and Cookie Management

Keeping state and tracking user activity across various pages and visits requires efficient and secure management of user sessions and cookies in web development. An additional critical component of authentication and security is efficient cookie and session management, which limits access to sensitive user information to those who need it.

Understanding Sessions and Cookies

Sessions are used to store information about a user across multiple HTTP requests. When a user accesses a server, the server creates a session for that user and assigns a unique identifier, usually stored in a cookie, which the client then sends in subsequent requests. The server, in turn, retrieves the session data using the identifier from the cookie, allowing it to maintain state over the stateless HTTP protocol.

Cookies are small pieces of data that servers send to the client, which the client stores and sends back to the server with each request. Cookies are the primary method for storing session identifiers on the client's side but can also store other useful data like user preferences.

Managing Cookie-Based User Sessions

Using the Go standard library, you can manage sessions by creating and setting cookies. Given below is a simple way to create a session and store the session ID in a cookie:

```
package main


import (
 "net/http"
 "github.com/gorilla/securecookie"
)
```

```
var hashKey = []byte("very-secret")
var s = securecookie.New(hashKey, nil)

func SetSession(w http.ResponseWriter, userID string) {
 encoded, err := s.Encode("session", map[string]string{
 "user_id": userID,
 })
 if err == nil {
 cookie := &http.Cookie{
 Name: "session",
 Value: encoded,
 Path: "/",
 HttpOnly: true, // HttpOnly is true so the cookie is not
accessible to JavaScript
 }
 http.SetCookie(w, cookie)
 }
}

func GetSession(r *http.Request) (userID string, err
error) {
 if cookie, err := r.Cookie("session"); err == nil {
```

```
cookieValue := make(map[string]string)
if err = s.Decode("session", cookie.Value,
&cookieValue); err == nil {
userID = cookieValue["user_id"]
}
}
return userID, err
}

func main() {
http.HandleFunc("/", func(w http.ResponseWriter, r
*http.Request) {
userID, _ := GetSession(r)
if userID != "" {
// User is logged in
w.Write([]byte("Welcome back, " + userID))
} else {
// User is not logged in
SetSession(w, "123456") // Suppose "123456" is our user
ID
w.Write([]byte("Session started!"))
}
```

```
  })
  http.ListenAndServe(":8080", nil)
}
```

In the above sample program, we use the **gorilla/securecookie** library for encoding and decoding cookie values securely. This library handles cookie security, such as ensuring that cookies are tamper-resistant.

Secure Session Management Techniques

Managing sessions securely involves several considerations to protect against common vulnerabilities:

- **Use HttpOnly and Secure Cookie Flags**: Setting the **HttpOnly** flag prevents client-side scripts from accessing the cookie, mitigating the risk of cross-site scripting (XSS) attacks. The **Secure** flag ensures that cookies are sent over HTTPS, protecting them from being intercepted during transmission.
- **Set Cookie Expiry and Max-Age**: Define when cookies should expire to reduce the risk of old cookies being used maliciously.
- **Regenerate Session IDs**: When a user's authentication state changes (e.g., logging in or out), regenerate the session ID. This prevents session fixation attacks, where an attacker fixes a user's session ID before the user logs in, then uses the session after the user has authenticated.
- **Use Secure Cookie Libraries**: As shown in the example, using libraries like **gorilla/securecookie** helps in securely encoding and decoding cookie data, ensuring that the contents cannot be easily tampered with.
- **Implement Proper Logout Mechanisms**: Ensure that logging out clears the session on both the client and server sides. This typically involves deleting the session data and clearing the session cookie.

Developers can keep their apps safe from common security risks and make them more user-friendly by using such above learned secure coding practices and strong session handling tools.

User registration and Password Management

Ensuring the security and integrity of users in web applications relies heavily on user registration and password management. Good password policies and efficient management work together to keep user data safe from prying eyes.

Creating System for User Registration and Password Mgmt

First things first: we create a basic system to securely store passwords and manage user registration. We will also go over ways to make sure that user accounts are secure by establishing strong password policies.

User Registration API

The user registration system will need to collect user data, validate it, and store it securely in a database. Given below is a basic structure for a user registration API:

```
package main


import (
 "encoding/json"
 "net/http"
 "golang.org/x/crypto/bcrypt"
)


type User struct {
 Username string `json:"username"`
 Password string `json:"password"`
}


// Dummy database store
var userDB = map[string]string{}
```

```
func main() {
 http.HandleFunc("/register", registerHandler)
 http.ListenAndServe(":8080", nil)
}

func registerHandler(w http.ResponseWriter, r
*http.Request) {
 var user User
 err := json.NewDecoder(r.Body).Decode(&user)
 if err != nil {
 http.Error(w, "Invalid request", http.StatusBadRequest)
 return
 }

 if _, exists := userDB[user.Username]; exists {
 http.Error(w, "Username already exists",
http.StatusBadRequest)
 return
 }

 hashedPassword, err :=
bcrypt.GenerateFromPassword([]byte(user.Password),
bcrypt.DefaultCost)
```

```
if err != nil {

http.Error(w, "Server error",
http.StatusInternalServerError)

return

}


userDB[user.Username] = string(hashedPassword)

w.WriteHeader(http.StatusCreated)

}
```

In this Go server code, we define a **`User`** type with a username and password. The **`registerHandler`** function handles user registration by hashing the password with bcrypt before storing it, which ensures that passwords are never stored in plaintext.

Managing and Protecting Passwords

When handling passwords, security is paramount. We use bcrypt, a robust hash function for securely hashing passwords. Bcrypt automatically incorporates a salt to protect against rainbow table attacks.

Following is why and how we use bcrypt:

- **Bcrypt Salting**: Bcrypt salts passwords automatically, which means it adds random data to the input before hashing it, ensuring that even identical passwords will have different hashes.
- **Bcrypt Work Factor**: The "cost" parameter in bcrypt allows you to set the computational cost of hashing, which can be configured to make it slower as hardware gets faster.

Defining Password Policies

To enhance security, defining and enforcing strong password policies is crucial. A good password policy might include the following rules:

- **Minimum Length**: Ensure passwords are at least 8 characters long.
- **Complexity Requirements**: Require a mix of uppercase letters, lowercase letters, numbers, and special characters.

- **No Common Passwords**: Check passwords against lists of common passwords to prevent the use of easily guessable passwords.

Implementing these above policies can be achieved during the registration process by adding validation steps as below:

```
func validatePassword(password string) bool {
 var (
 hasMinLen = false
 hasUpper = false
 hasLower = false
 hasNumber = false
 hasSpecial = false
 )

 hasMinLen = len(password) >= 8
 for _, char := range password {
 switch {
 case unicode.IsUpper(char):
 hasUpper = true
 case unicode.IsLower(char):
 hasLower = true
 case unicode.IsDigit(char):
 hasNumber = true
 case unicode.IsPunct(char) || unicode.IsSymbol(char):
```

```
hasSpecial = true
}
}

return hasMinLen && hasUpper && hasLower && hasNumber &&
hasSpecial
}
```

This above function checks if a password meets the defined criteria, including length and character variety. You would call this function in your registration handler to enforce these policies.

These above discussed and implemented practices help protect against common vulnerabilities and attacks, providing a safer environment for users to interact with the application.

Rate Limiting and Abuse Prevention

When it comes to web applications, rate limiting is an essential reliability and security measure for preventing abuse and keeping services available in high-traffic or attack situations like Distributed Denial of Service (DDoS) assaults. To prevent the backend infrastructure of a service like gitforgits.com from being overloaded, rate limiting is used to control the rate at which user requests are processed.

Understanding Rate Limiting

Rate limiting controls the number of times a user can make a request to a server in a specific period. It is often implemented to:

- **Prevent abuse and misuse**: Ensuring that APIs and services are not misused (e.g., for spam or brute force attacks).
- **Limit resource consumption**: Preventing one user from consuming all available resources, thus ensuring fair use among all users.
- **Mitigate DDoS attacks**: Reducing the effectiveness of attempts to flood the server with high volumes of requests, thereby maintaining availability.

Implementing Custom Rate Limiting

There are various ways to implement rate limiting, such as using a fixed window counter, a sliding window log, or a token bucket algorithm. In the below program, we will use a simple in-memory rate limiter for demonstration purposes using a token bucket approach, which offers a good balance between complexity and effectiveness.

Define Rate Limiter Structure

We will create a basic rate limiter using Go's standard library components:

```
package main

import (
 "fmt"
 "net/http"
 "sync"
 "time"
)

type RateLimiter struct {
 visits map[string]int
 mtx sync.Mutex
}

func NewRateLimiter() *RateLimiter {
 return &RateLimiter{
 visits: make(map[string]int),
```

```
 }
}

func (rl *RateLimiter) Limit(next http.Handler)
http.Handler {
 return http.HandlerFunc(func(w http.ResponseWriter, r
*http.Request) {
 rl.mtx.Lock()
 defer rl.mtx.Unlock()

 clientIP := r.RemoteAddr
 if _, ok := rl.visits[clientIP]; !ok {
 rl.visits[clientIP] = 0
 }
 rl.visits[clientIP]++

 if rl.visits[clientIP] > 100 { // Allow 100 requests per
hour
 http.Error(w, "Rate limit exceeded",
http.StatusTooManyRequests)
 return
 }
```

```
 next.ServeHTTP(w, r)
 })
}

func main() {
 mux := http.NewServeMux()
 mux.HandleFunc("/", func(w http.ResponseWriter, r
*http.Request) {
 fmt.Fprintln(w, "Welcome to gitforgits.com")
 })

 limiter := NewRateLimiter()
 wrappedMux := limiter.Limit(mux)

 http.ListenAndServe(":8080", wrappedMux)
}
```

This implementation uses a simple map to track the number of requests per IP address and blocks any IP that exceeds the limit. It is synchronized using a mutex to prevent race conditions.

Integrating Rate Limiting

In the provided example, the **RateLimiter** middleware wraps the main HTTP handler. It checks if the number of requests from an IP exceeds a set limit (100 requests per hour in this sample program) and blocks further requests by sending a **429 Too Many Requests** HTTP status.

Protecting against DDoS Attacks

In the context of a DDoS attack where multiple systems might attempt to flood the server with requests, this rate limiting mechanism can significantly mitigate the impact. By limiting the number of requests an individual IP can make:

- **Reduces server load**: The server only needs to handle a predefined number of requests per IP, preventing resource exhaustion.
- **Maintains availability**: By preventing abusive traffic patterns, legitimate users continue to access the service without degradation.

While the simple rate limiter shown here is useful for understanding basic concepts and small-scale applications, a production environment would likely require a more robust solution. Advanced implementations might use distributed rate limiting where state is shared across multiple servers or services, possibly integrating with cloud-based security services that provide automatic scaling and DDoS mitigation strategies.

Summary

We covered the difficult but important subject of user authentication and web application security in this chapter. First, we covered the fundamentals of user authentication, getting a feel for how it works and why it's important for protecting sensitive information on the web. This prepared the groundwork for delving into more specialized mechanisms such as OAuth2 and JWTs, which are critical for modern authentication strategies involving third-party providers. We looked into OAuth2, which is a framework for authentication that lets users use their existing social media accounts, such as Google's, to log in. After that, we put JWTs into place, which allowed for the safe transfer of data between parties using small, self-contained JSON objects.

Managing sessions and cookies was also addressed in the chapter, with an emphasis on securely handling user sessions through cookies. The chapter went into detail about creating a bespoke API for user registration and password management, with an emphasis on securely managing passwords using modern hashing algorithms.

At last, we learned the art of rate limiting and abuse prevention, two crucial safeguards against malicious automated access and distributed denial of service (DDoS) assaults. As part of this process, we built a custom rate limiting mechanism to regulate the maximum number of requests per second. This limits the potential for abuse and keeps the service up and running even when attacked or under heavy load.

In sum, we learned some useful skills for securing our Go applications, managing sessions securely, and implementing advanced user authentication methods in this chapter.

CHAPTER 5: INTEGRATING DATABASES WITH GORM

Chapter Overview

In this chapter, we will go over how to use GORM, a strong Object-Relational Mapping (ORM) tool for Go, to integrate databases into web applications. GORM facilitates database interactions by converting complicated SQL commands into This chapter will walk you through every step of using GORM to create and manage databases.

First of all, we will go over some criteria to keep in mind when choosing a database, including GORM compatibility, ease of use, and scalability. Our next stop is GORM for ORM setup, where we will show you how to incorporate GORM into your Go project and configure it to connect to your preferred database. In order to use GORM's features to streamline database operations, this configuration is required.

Next, we will go over connecting to SQL databases, specifically how to use GORM to create a safe and efficient connection between your Go app and the database server. Things like connection pooling, handling configuration settings, and best practices for keeping a stable connection are all part of this. We will delve deeply into GORM's database CRUD operations, which include reading, updating, and deleting records. Here we will show you some code examples and go over how GORM converts them into SQL queries. You will also discover how to use GORM's advanced features, like scopes and hooks, to modify and expand the ORM's capabilities to suit complicated business logic, make code more reusable, and improve query efficiency.

The next topic will be database migration management, necessary for updating, enhancing, and preserving the database schema without causing downtime. As your application develops, we will show you how to use the migration tools in GORM to make safe changes to the database schema. Ensuring data integrity and consistency is crucial in applications that handle multiple simultaneous database operations. This chapter also addresses transactions and concurrency control. We will also go over some techniques for managing transactions in GORM and some strategies to stay away from common problems like deadlocks and race conditions.

Through the completion of this chapter, you will have a solid understanding of GORM database integration and management in web applications. This will allow you to build scalable and robust web applications with efficient data management and operations.

Setting up GORM for ORM

An effective means of communication between developers and databases is given by the widely used GORM Object-Relational Mapping (ORM) library. The GORM package simplifies CRUD operations and dealing with relationships between database entities by transforming complicated SQL commands into straightforward Go methods.

Introduction to GORM

GORM stands for "Go ORM". As an ORM library, GORM allows for the handling of relational database interactions in an object-oriented manner. This means you can work with database records as Go structs, reducing the amount of manual SQL you have to write and helping maintain clean and maintainable code.

Following are the key components of GORM:

- **Models**: In GORM, models are Go structs that correspond to tables in your database. Each field in the struct usually corresponds to a column in the table.
- **DB Connection Handler**: GORM provides a **`*gorm.DB`** object which is used to perform database operations. This object handles all tasks related to database communication.
- **Migration Tools**: GORM can automatically migrate your database schema based on your models. This is extremely useful during development, as it simplifies the process of updating the database schema as your application evolves.
- **Association Handling**: GORM handles foreign keys and relationships (one-to-one, many-to-one, many-to-many) natively, making it easier to deal with related data.
- **Hooks**: GORM allows developers to define custom logic to be executed at different points in the lifecycle of a model (e.g., before or after creating a record).

Setting up GORM in Development Environment

To set up GORM in your Go project, you need to install the GORM package, configure it to connect to your database, and set up your models.

Install GORM

To get started, you need to install GORM and the database driver for your database of choice. Since we're using PostgreSQL, you'll need the GORM library and its PostgreSQL driver:

```
go get -u gorm.io/gorm

go get -u gorm.io/driver/postgres
```

Connect to the Database

To use GORM with your PostgreSQL database, you need to establish a connection using GORM's database driver. Given below is how you can do it:

```
package main

```

```
import (
 "gorm.io/gorm"
 "gorm.io/driver/postgres"
 "log"
)

func main() {
 dsn := "host=localhost user=myuser dbname=mydb
sslmode=disable password=mypassword"
 db, err := gorm.Open(postgres.Open(dsn), &gorm.Config{})
 if err != nil {
 log.Fatalf("Failed to connect to database: %v", err)
 }
 log.Println("Connected to database")
}
```

This above code snippet creates a connection to a PostgreSQL database. The **dsn** (data source name) string contains information needed to connect to the database, such as the host, user, database name, SSL mode, and password.

Define Models

After establishing a connection, define your models. For example, if you have a **Book** model, you might define it like this:

```
type Book struct {
 gorm.Model
```

```
 Title string
 Author string
 Description string
}
```

Perform Migrations

GORM can automatically create and update tables in your database according to your models. You can perform migrations like this:

```
db.AutoMigrate(&Book{})
```

This will check your database and ensure that it matches the schema defined by your models, creating or altering tables as necessary.

Not only does this GORM simplify your database interactions by hiding the complexities of raw SQL commands, but it also comes with a plethora of features to manage data relationships, schema migrations, and retrieval and manipulation of data.

Database Selection for Application

Selecting the right database is a critical decision for any application, impacting performance, scalability, and maintenance. For Go applications, the choice often hinges on several factors including the nature of the data, the scale of the application, and the existing ecosystem.

Common Databases used in Go Apps

1. **PostgreSQL**: A powerful, open-source object-relational database system known for its reliability, feature robustness, and performance. It supports complex queries, foreign keys, joins, views, and stored procedures.
2. **MySQL**: Another popular open-source relational database. It is known for its ease of use and speed, making it suitable for applications with less complex query requirements.
3. **SQLite**: A lightweight, file-based database, embedded into the end program. It's a good choice for small applications, testing environments, or simple applications not requiring a standalone database server.
4. **MongoDB**: A leading NoSQL database, known for its high performance, high availability, and easy scalability. It's ideal for applications with large volumes of unstructured data.

5. **Redis**: An open-source (BSD licensed), in-memory data structure store, used as a database, cache, and message broker. It supports data structures such as strings, hashes, lists, sets, and sorted sets.

Choosing PostgreSQL

For **`gitforgits.com`**, considering the need for robust transaction support, complex querying capabilities, and strong consistency, PostgreSQL is an excellent choice. It integrates well with GORM, providing a powerful toolkit for ORM that leverages Go's features to facilitate database interactions.

Designing Database Schema

The next step is to design the database schema for **`gitforgits.com`**. Suppose our application needs to handle books, authors, and user transactions, then following is a simplified schema:

- **Books**: Contains details about the books.
- **Authors**: Stores author details. A book can have multiple authors.
- **Users**: User details who can log in and make transactions.
- **Transactions**: Records transactions or purchases made by the users.

```
CREATE TABLE authors (
 id SERIAL PRIMARY KEY,
 name VARCHAR(100) NOT NULL,
 bio TEXT
);

CREATE TABLE books (
 id SERIAL PRIMARY KEY,
 title VARCHAR(255) NOT NULL,
 description TEXT,
 author_id INTEGER,
```

```
 FOREIGN KEY (author_id) REFERENCES authors (id)
);

CREATE TABLE users (
 id SERIAL PRIMARY KEY,
 username VARCHAR(50) UNIQUE NOT NULL,
 password_hash TEXT NOT NULL,
 email VARCHAR(100) UNIQUE NOT NULL
);

CREATE TABLE transactions (
 id SERIAL PRIMARY KEY,
 user_id INTEGER NOT NULL,
 book_id INTEGER NOT NULL,
 transaction_date TIMESTAMP DEFAULT CURRENT_TIMESTAMP,
 FOREIGN KEY (user_id) REFERENCES users (id),
 FOREIGN KEY (book_id) REFERENCES books (id)
);
```

Integrating PostgreSQL with GORM

After setting up the database schema, integrating it with GORM involves defining corresponding models. Following is how you could set up basic models for **gitforgits.com** using GORM:

```
package main
```

```
import (
 "gorm.io/driver/postgres"
 "gorm.io/gorm"
)

type Author struct {
 gorm.Model
 Name string
 Bio string
 Books []Book
}

type Book struct {
 gorm.Model
 Title string
 Description string
 AuthorID uint
}

type User struct {
```

```
 gorm.Model

 Username string

 PasswordHash string

 Email string

}


type Transaction struct {

 gorm.Model

 UserID uint

 BookID uint

 TransactionDate time.Time

}


func main() {

 dsn := "host=localhost user=postgres dbname=gitforgits
sslmode=disable password=yourpassword"

 db, err := gorm.Open(postgres.Open(dsn), &gorm.Config{})

 if err != nil {

 panic("failed to connect database")

 }


 // Migrate the schema
```

```
 db.AutoMigrate(&Author{}, &Book{}, &User{},
&Transaction{})

}
```

This setup involves defining Go structs mapped to the tables in PostgreSQL and using GORM to connect to the database and migrate schemas based on the struct definitions. GORM's **AutoMigrate** function helps create and update tables according to the model.

Database CRUD Operations

CRUD operations, an acronym for Create, Read, Update, and Delete, are fundamental for interacting with databases in any application. Using GORM with PostgreSQL, we can streamline these operations by leveraging GORM's ORM capabilities to work with Go objects that map directly to database tables.

Setting up the Environment

To demonstrate CRUD operations, we assume you already have GORM and PostgreSQL configured as described previously. We will use a simple **Book** model for our examples.

Following is the Go struct for the **Book** model, which GORM will use to perform operations on the corresponding database table:

```
package main


import (
 "gorm.io/gorm"
 "gorm.io/driver/postgres"
 "log"
)


type Book struct {
```

```
 gorm.Model
 Title string
 Author string
 Description string
}

func main() {
 dsn := "host=localhost user=myuser dbname=mydb
sslmode=disable password=mypassword"
 db, err := gorm.Open(postgres.Open(dsn), &gorm.Config{})
 if err != nil {
 log.Fatalf("Failed to connect to database: %v", err)
 }

 // Auto migrate our schema
 db.AutoMigrate(&Book{})
}
```

This code snippet sets up a **Book** model and ensures the database schema is created or migrated properly.

CRUD Operations in GORM

Create (Inserting Data)

To add a new book to the database:

```
func createBook(db *gorm.DB, title, author, description
string) {
 book := Book{Title: title, Author: author, Description:
description}
 result := db.Create(&book) // Pass pointer of data to
Create


 if result.Error != nil {
 log.Printf("Error creating book: %v", result.Error)
 return
 }


 log.Printf("Book created: %v", book)
}
```

This function takes a database connection and book details, creates a **Book** struct, and inserts it into the database.

Read (Querying Data)

To read books from the database:

```
func getBooks(db *gorm.DB) {
 var books []Book
 result := db.Find(&books) // Find all books


 if result.Error != nil {
```

```
 log.Printf("Error finding books: %v", result.Error)
 return
 }

 for _, book := range books {
 log.Printf("Book: %+v", book)
 }
}
```

This function retrieves all books stored in the database.

Update (Modifying Data)

To update a book:

```
func updateBook(db *gorm.DB, bookID uint, title,
description string) {
 var book Book
 result := db.First(&book, bookID) // Find the book by ID

 if result.Error != nil {
 log.Printf("Error finding book: %v", result.Error)
 return
 }

 book.Title = title
```

```
 book.Description = description
 db.Save(&book)


 log.Printf("Book updated: %+v", book)
}
```

This function finds a book by its ID and updates its title and description.

Delete (Removing Data)

To delete a book:

```
func deleteBook(db *gorm.DB, bookID uint) {
 var book Book
 result := db.First(&book, bookID) // Find the book by ID


 if result.Error != nil {
 log.Printf("Error finding book: %v", result.Error)
 return
 }


 db.Delete(&book)
 log.Printf("Book deleted: %+v", book)
}
```

This function deletes a book from the database by its ID. By mapping Go structs to database tables, GORM allows developers to work with database entities as if they were regular Go objects, significantly simplifying database interactions. These operations form the backbone of most web applications, enabling dynamic data management and interaction.

Advanced GORM Features

GORM, as a feature-rich ORM for Go, offers various advanced features that can enhance how we manage database interactions in web applications like gitforgits.com. Two of these powerful features are Hooks and Scopes, which allow for more fine-grained control over queries and the lifecycle of model operations.

Understanding Hooks in GORM

Hooks in GORM are methods that get automatically called when certain actions occur on a model, similar to callbacks or events in other programming frameworks. These hooks can be used to execute logic before or after creating, updating, deleting, or querying a model. This functionality is extremely useful for handling tasks like data validation, cleanup, or logging.

Commonly Used GORM Hooks

Following are some of the hooks provided by GORM:

- **BeforeCreate, AfterCreate**: Called before and after inserting a record.
- **BeforeUpdate, AfterUpdate**: Called before and after updating a record.
- **BeforeDelete, AfterDelete**: Called before and after deleting a record.
- **BeforeSave, AfterSave**: Called before and after saving a record (create or update).
- **BeforeFind, AfterFind**: Called before and after retrieving a record.

Sample Program: Implementing a Hook

Suppose we want to log every time a book is updated in our database. We can use the **BeforeUpdate** hook for the **Book** model:

```
type Book struct {
 gorm.Model
 Title string
 Author string
 Description string
```

```
}

func (book *Book) BeforeUpdate(tx *gorm.DB) (err error) {
 log.Printf("Updating book: %s", book.Title)
 return nil
}
```

In the above sample program, every time a **Book** is about to be updated, it logs a message.

Understanding Scopes in GORM

Scopes are a way to encapsulate common queries in GORM to reuse them easily across your application. A scope is essentially a function that takes a ***gorm.DB** instance and returns a modified ***gorm.DB** instance, which can be chained with other queries.

Let's say we often need to fetch books by a particular author. We can define a scope to simplify this operation:

```
func BooksByAuthor(author string) func(db *gorm.DB)
*gorm.DB {
 return func(db *gorm.DB) *gorm.DB {
 return db.Where("author = ?", author)
 }
}
```

You can use this scope in your queries like so:

```
var books []Book
db.Scopes(BooksByAuthor("J.K. Rowling")).Find(&books)
```

This scope filters the books by the author "J.K. Rowling".

Putting Hooks and Scopes into Practice

We will see how we might integrate both hooks and scopes in gitforgits.com, particularly focusing on logging and custom queries.

Auto-Logging Changes

Suppose we want to automatically log changes not just for updates but also when books are created or deleted. We could expand our hook usage like this:

```
func (book *Book) AfterCreate(tx *gorm.DB) (err error) {

 log.Printf("Book created: %s", book.Title)

 return nil

}


func (book *Book) AfterDelete(tx *gorm.DB) (err error) {

 log.Printf("Book deleted: %s", book.Title)

 return nil

}
```

Advanced Scopes for Complex Queries

And, now consider you need a complex query that filters books by a certain publication date range and a specific author. We can create a combined scope for this:

```
func RecentBooksByAuthor(author string, from, to
time.Time) func(db *gorm.DB) *gorm.DB {

 return func(db *gorm.DB) *gorm.DB {

 return db.Where("author = ? AND created_at BETWEEN ? AND
?", author, from, to)

 }
```

```
}
```

This can then be used as:

```
var recentBooks []Book

db.Scopes(RecentBooksByAuthor("J.K. Rowling",
time.Now().AddDate(-1, 0, 0),
time.Now())).Find(&recentBooks)
```

Taken as a whole, these capabilities have the potential to significantly simplify approaches to data management.

Managing Database Migrations

Understanding Database Migrations

Database migrations involve modifying the database schema over time to accommodate changes in the application's data model. This might include adding new tables, changing existing tables, or dropping tables. Migrations ensure that these changes can be applied in a controlled and versioned manner. The GORM provides built-in support for database migrations, which simplifies updating the database schema without having to manually write SQL scripts.

GORM's Migration Features

GORM's migration features offer several advantages:

- Automatically apply schema changes to the database based on model definitions.
- Reduce the risk of losing data by handling migrations programmatically.
- Keep track of changes in the schema alongside the application code, facilitating easier deployments and rollbacks.

Sample Program: Migration with GORM

To demonstrate GORM's migration capabilities, we consider a scenario where we initially have a **Book** model and later decide to add an **Author** model that references **Book**.

Initial Setup

First, we define the **Book** model and perform the initial migration to create the corresponding table in the database.

```
package main

import (
 "gorm.io/driver/postgres"
 "gorm.io/gorm"
 "log"
)

type Book struct {
 gorm.Model
 Title string
 Description string
}

func main() {
 dsn := "host=localhost user=youruser dbname=yourdb
sslmode=disable password=yourpassword"
 db, err := gorm.Open(postgres.Open(dsn), &gorm.Config{})
 if err != nil {
 log.Fatalf("Failed to connect to database: %v", err)
 }
```

```
    // Automatically migrate our schema
    db.AutoMigrate(&Book{})
}
```

Adding New Model with Relationships

Suppose our application requirements evolve, and we need to add an **Author** model that has a one-to-many relationship with **Book**.

```
type Author struct {
    gorm.Model
    Name string
    Books []Book `gorm:"foreignKey:AuthorID"`
}

type Book struct {
    gorm.Model
    Title string
    Description string
    AuthorID uint
}
```

Now, we need to update our migration logic to accommodate this new model.

```
func main() {
    dsn := "host=localhost user=youruser dbname=yourdb
```

```
sslmode=disable password=yourpassword"
 db, err := gorm.Open(postgres.Open(dsn), &gorm.Config{})
 if err != nil {
 log.Fatalf("Failed to connect to database: %v", err)
 }

 // Migrate the schema with the new Author model
 db.AutoMigrate(&Author{}, &Book{})
}
```

Modifying Existing Schema

We will further assume we need to add a new field to the **Book** model, such as a **PublishYear**:

```
type Book struct {
 gorm.Model
 Title string
 Description string
 AuthorID uint
 PublishYear int
}
```

Again, you would run the **AutoMigrate** function to apply these changes:

```
func main() {
 // Your database connection setup
```

```
 // Automatically migrate our schema
 db.AutoMigrate(&Author{}, &Book{})
}
```

In such applications, conflicts or issues also might arise during migrations, such as data type changes that could lead to data loss. GORM does allow for custom migration strategies using migration hooks or manual migrations where you provide specific SQL commands to handle complex changes safely.

Transactions and Concurrency Control

Understanding Transactions

A transaction in a database context is a sequence of operations performed as a single logical unit of work. If any of the operations fail, the transaction fails, and the database state is left unchanged. GORM supports transactions out of the box, allowing developers to group operations that need to be executed together. To guarantee data integrity and application dependability, any strong web app must manage transactions and handle concurrency control. Conversely, concurrency control makes sure that transactions that happen at the same time don't hurt each other.

Using GORM to Manage Transactions

Given below is how you can use GORM to handle transactions effectively:

```
package main

import (
 "gorm.io/driver/postgres"
 "gorm.io/gorm"
 "log"
)
```

```
func main() {
 dsn := "host=localhost user=myuser dbname=mydb
sslmode=disable password=mypassword"
 db, err := gorm.Open(postgres.Open(dsn), &gorm.Config{})
 if err != nil {
 log.Fatal("failed to connect database")
 }

 // Transaction start
 err = db.Transaction(func(tx *gorm.DB) error {
 // Perform a series of operations within the transaction
 if err := tx.Create(&Book{Title: "New Book",
Description: "Description of new book"}).Error; err !=
nil {
 // Return any error will rollback
 return err
 }

 if err := tx.Create(&Author{Name: "New Author"}).Error;
err != nil {
 // Return any error will rollback
 return err
 }
```

```
// Return nil will commit the whole transaction
return nil
})

if err != nil {
log.Println("Transaction failed:", err)
}
}
```

In the above sample program, we wrap our database operations within **`db.Transaction()`**. This ensures that if any of the operations within the transaction block fail, the entire transaction will roll back to the initial state, maintaining data integrity.

Concurrency Control

Concurrency control is about managing simultaneous operations without leading to inconsistencies. Common issues include:

- **Lost updates**: Occurs when two or more transactions are updating the same data simultaneously, and one of the updates overwrites others.
- **Dirty reads**: Happens when a transaction reads data that is being updated by another ongoing transaction.
- **Non-repeatable reads and phantom reads**: Occur due to reading updated data or newly inserted data in a repeated read.

Managing Concurrency

To manage concurrency, GORM provides several options, including the use of **`Optimistic Locking`** with a version field. Given below is how to set it up:

```
type Product struct {
```

```
gorm.Model
Name string
Code string
Price uint
Version int `gorm:"default:1"`
}
```

Whenever you update an instance of **Product**, increment the **Version**:

```
func updateProductPrice(db *gorm.DB, productID uint,
newPrice uint) error {
 result := db.Model(&Product{}).Where("id = ? AND version
= ?", productID, 1).Updates(map[string]interface{}{
 "price": newPrice,
 "version": gorm.Expr("version + ?", 1),
 })
 if result.RowsAffected == 0 {
 return errors.New("update failed due to concurrent
update")
 }
 return nil
}
```

This approach ensures that updates to a product are not overwritten by other concurrent transactions, preventing lost updates. Overall, GORM provides robust tools for managing transaction and concurrency control aspects, ensuring that data handling is reliable and efficient.

Summary

In conclusion, this chapter covered all the bases for using this strong ORM tool with Go applications, with an emphasis on the database integration with GORM. We started by looking at various databases that are often used in Go applications, then we compared their benefits and finally settled on PostgreSQL because of its stability and compatibility with GORM. We next proceeded to configure GORM so that it would work well with the database that we had chosen. This setup included defining models that represent database tables and using GORM's auto-migration capabilities to keep the database schema in sync with the models.

After that, we went on to CRUD operations, where we learned how to use GORM's methods to manipulate database entries. These operations made the code more readable and easier to maintain by reducing complicated SQL tasks to manageable Go methods. Advanced GORM features like scopes and hooks were also covered. We showed that logic can be executed at different points in the model lifecycle using hooks, and that scopes can clean up the codebase by refining queries and encapsulating common database interactions.

Database migration management was another important topic. We looked at how GORM makes it easy to migrate database schemas without having to write any SQL scripts by hand and guarantees that the database will automatically reflect any changes made to the application's data models. Concurrency control and transactions were our last topics. We showed how GORM manages transactions to guarantee consistent and accurate data. In addition, we went over the GORM concurrency control mechanisms that help handle concurrent database operations and avoid typical problems that arise from them.

CHAPTER 6: CREATING MICROSERVICES IN GO

Chapter Overview

This chapter explores the process of creating microservices, a method that is gaining popularity because it improves software architectures in terms of scalability, flexibility, and resilience. In this chapter, we will cover the basics of microservices and how to design, implement, and manage them effectively. We begin with the design principles for microservices, which lay the foundational concepts and best practices essential for building robust microservice architectures. The next step is to learn the mechanics of establishing a microservices framework. In order to facilitate the deployment and scalability of microservices, it is necessary to configure the development and production environments.

A key feature of microservices architectures is inter-service communication and so we will cover the basics of RESTful APIs and go into more advanced techniques like gRPC. A comprehensive study of gRPC and protocol buffers will be done. We will teach you how to use Protocol Buffers to define service interfaces and message structures, and how gRPC uses these definitions to make type-safe, low-latency communication between services. Another crucial topic is the implementation of API gateways.

All clients access the API through an API gateway, which also handles failures, adds an extra layer of security, and routes requests to the right microservice. We will also go over how to authenticate and authorize microservices. Among these topics is the need of addressing security patterns in microservice architectures to prevent unauthorized access to services. Lastly, we will explore Kubernetes and its capabilities in containerizing microservices.

This chapter will teach all you need to know about microservices, from design to implementation to maintenance, so they can create resilient applications that can scale to meet the demands of modern software.

Design Principles for Microservices

In microservices architecture, a single application is built out of several smaller services. These services communicate with one another using lightweight mechanisms, such as an HTTP-based API. Each service runs in its own process. Deployment, scaling, and updates can be handled independently by each service, which is built around a specific business capability. If you want to know how to build microservices, you need to know the core design principles as below:

- Decomposition by Business Capability
- Independence and Decentralization
- Failure Isolation
- Automate Everything
- Observability

Decomposition by Business Capability

Microservices are organized around business capabilities, where each service performs a single business function. This principle supports modularity, making it easier to understand, develop, and test the application. For example, decomposing services by functionality (e.g., user management, product handling, order processing) ensures that changes in one area of the business impact only the related microservice. This localized impact reduces the complexity of updates and minimizes the risk of disrupting the entire system.

Independence and Decentralization

Each microservice is developed, deployed, and scaled independently from the others. This means using different technology stacks and data storage solutions that are best suited to each service's needs, and not being constrained by the choices made for other services.

For example, the order processing service might use a different database system more suited to transactions than the product catalog service. This flexibility enhances developer productivity and service performance.

Failure Isolation

One of the significant advantages of microservices is that a failure in one service doesn't necessarily bring down the whole system. Each service should be designed to handle failures gracefully and, where possible, continue to operate in a degraded mode if dependent services are unavailable.

So for example, if on **gitforgits.com**, if the payment service fails, the product browsing and cart services can continue to function, albeit without completing purchases. This isolation helps maintain a better overall user experience even in the face of partial system failures.

Automate Everything

Automation is a key enabler of microservices, covering areas from testing and deployment to scaling and recovery. Continuous integration and deployment (CI/CD) practices are integral, allowing frequent and reliable changes to be made to the services.

Observability

With many services working together, it's vital to have robust monitoring, logging, and diagnostic capabilities. Observability involves understanding the state of the system by examining its outputs. Effective logging, metrics collection, and tracing are crucial. It means a lot to our project for issues to be quickly identified and rectified, often before they impact users. It allows for performance optimizations based on real usage data and can help predict future system needs.

These above design principles allow for rapid development cycles, robust performance, and superior fault tolerance, all while keeping complexity manageable. By adhering to these principles, the project can ensure that its microservices architecture delivers its full potential benefits.

Setting up Microservices Environment

Introduction to Gin Framework

The Gin framework is a high-performance HTTP web framework written in Go that is designed for building microservices due to its efficiency and simplicity. It offers a robust set of features that can enhance the development of microservices by providing a powerful routing mechanism, middleware support, and the ability to easily manage JSON rendering, making it well-suited for building efficient and scalable REST APIs.

Gin is celebrated for its performance and is one of the fastest web frameworks available for Go. This performance advantage is due to its use of the **`httprouter`** package, which provides quick look-up of routes, a critical feature for services handling high volumes of requests. It also simplifies error handling and supports middleware, allowing developers to add reusable components that intercept HTTP requests efficiently.

Capabilities of Gin

- **Efficient Routing**: Gin uses a custom version of **`httprouter`**, making it incredibly fast, which is vital for services that require high-performance characteristics.
- **Middleware Support**: Allows developers to plug in functions that can be executed before or after requests; this is useful for tasks like logging, authorization, and metrics collection.
- **Error Management**: Gin provides a convenient way to collect and manage errors encountered during HTTP request processing.
- **JSON Validation**: Supports binding and validation of JSON inputs, reducing boilerplate code and simplifying the handling of input validation.
- **Great Developer Experience**: With features like hot reloading, comprehensive logging, and detailed debug outputs, Gin enhances developer productivity.

Setting up Gin for gotforgits.com

To begin using Gin for developing microservices, you first need to set up your development environment. This includes installing the Gin package, setting up a basic server, and preparing the environment for development of a microservice.

Install Gin

You can add Gin to your Go project by running the following command in your terminal:

```
go get -u github.com/gin-gonic/gin
```

Create a Basic Gin Server

To create a basic server with Gin, you start by importing the Gin package and setting up the HTTP routes. Below is a simple example that shows how to set up a Gin server:

```
package main

import (
 "github.com/gin-gonic/gin"
 "net/http"
)

func main() {
 router := gin.Default() // Create a Gin router with
default middleware: logger and recovery (crash-free)
middleware

 // Define a simple route
 router.GET("/", func(c *gin.Context) {
 c.JSON(http.StatusOK, gin.H{
 "message": "Hello world!",
 })
 })
```

```
 // Start serving the application
 router.Run(":8080") // By default, it will listen on
port 8080
}
```

In this code, **gin.Default()** initializes a Gin engine with the logger and recovery middleware attached. The **GET** method defines a route that simply returns a JSON response with a "Hello world!" message. The **Run** function starts the HTTP server on port 8080.

Test Your Setup

After setting up your Gin server, you can test it by navigating to **http://localhost:8080/** in your web browser or using a tool like curl:

```
curl http://localhost:8080/
```

This command should return a JSON response:

```
{"message": "Hello world!"}
```

Also note that the simplicity of Gin also helps in reducing the learning curve and speeding up the development process, providing an all-around efficient development experience.

Inter-service Communication with REST and gRPC

Overview

In a microservices architecture, services are designed to be loosely coupled yet must interact with each other to function as a cohesive application. Inter-service communication is thus a critical component, determining how services exchange data and invoke functionalities amongst themselves. Effective communication strategies ensure services can be independently developed, deployed, and scaled while maintaining robustness and flexibility in the overall application architecture.

Inter-service communication strategies impact the application's performance, reliability, and scalability. Poor communication patterns can lead to bottlenecks, increased latencies, and heightened complexity in handling data consistency and fault tolerance.

Efficient communication protocols help in achieving:

1. **Decoupling**: Services should operate independently, with minimal knowledge about each other's internal workings.
2. **Scalability**: The system should manage increased loads by scaling services independently.
3. **Resilience**: The failure of one service should not incapacitate others.
4. **Maintainability**: Easier to update and maintain services due to isolated changes.

Choosing Communication Protocols: REST vs. gRPC

Two popular methods for implementing inter-service communication are REST (Representational State Transfer) and gRPC (gRPC Remote Procedure Calls). Each comes with its own strengths and is suited to different scenarios.

REST for Inter-service Communication

REST uses standard HTTP methods and is based on a stateless, client-server, cacheable communications protocol -- the standard web HTTP. It's most suitable for public APIs and web services, where wide compatibility and flexibility are required.

Advantages:

- Easy to understand and implement.
- HTTP support is ubiquitous, and REST can be used with any data format.
- Responses can be cached based on HTTP headers.

gRPC for Inter-service Communication

gRPC is a modern, high-performance framework that can run in any environment. It uses HTTP/2 for transport, Protocol Buffers as the interface definition language, and provides features like authentication, load balancing, and bidirectional streaming.

Advantages:

- gRPC is designed for low latency and high throughput.
- API interfaces defined using Protocol Buffers ensure consistent implementations across services.
- gRPC supports streaming requests and responses, ideal for real-time communication.

Setting up REST and gRPC

To demonstrate both REST and gRPC, we set up two microservices: one providing a service and the other consuming it. We will use Go with the Gin framework for REST and the official gRPC library for gRPC.

Install Necessary Packages

- First, ensure you have the necessary packages:

```
# For Gin (REST)
go get -u github.com/gin-gonic/gin

# For gRPC and Protocol Buffers
go get -u google.golang.org/grpc
go get -u google.golang.org/protobuf
```

- We will create two services as below:
    - A **ProductService** that will be available over both REST and gRPC.
    - A **ClientService** that consumes the **ProductService**.

Creating ProductService with REST

Following is how to set up a simple REST server using Gin:

```
package main

import (
 "github.com/gin-gonic/gin"
 "net/http"
)

func main() {
```

```
 router := gin.Default()
 router.GET("/products", func(c *gin.Context) {
 c.JSON(http.StatusOK, gin.H{"products": []string{"Book",
"Pen"}})
 })
 router.Run(":8080")
}
```

Creating ProductService with gRPC

- Define the gRPC service using Protocol Buffers:

```
syntax = "proto3";

package product;

service ProductService {
 rpc ListProducts (Empty) returns (ProductResponse) {}
}

message Empty {}

message ProductResponse {
 repeated string products = 1;
}
```

- Generate the Go code from the Protocol Buffer definition, then implement the server:

```
package main

import (
 "context"
 "log"
 "net"

 "google.golang.org/grpc"
 pb "path/to/your/protobuf/package"
)

type server struct {
 pb.UnimplementedProductServiceServer
}

func (s *server) ListProducts(ctx context.Context, in
*pb.Empty) (*pb.ProductResponse, error) {
 return &pb.ProductResponse{Products: []string{"Book",
"Pen"}}, nil
}
```

```
func main() {
 lis, err := net.Listen("tcp", ":9090")
 if err != nil {
 log.Fatalf("failed to listen: %v", err)
 }
 s := grpc.NewServer()
 pb.RegisterProductServiceServer(s, &server{})
 if err := s.Serve(lis); err != nil {
 log.Fatalf("failed to serve: %v", err)
 }
}
```

Creating ClientService

- For the REST client:

```
package main

import (
 "log"
 "net/http"
 "io/ioutil"
)
```

```
func main() {
 resp, err := http.Get("http://localhost:8080/products")
 if err != nil {
 log.Fatal(err)
 }
 defer resp.Body.Close()
 body, err := ioutil.ReadAll(resp.Body)
 if err != nil {
 log.Fatal(err)
 }
 log.Println(string(body))
}
```

- For the gRPC client:

```
package main

import (
 "context"
 "log"
 "google.golang.org/grpc"
 pb "path/to/your/protobuf/package"
)
```

```
func main() {

 conn, err := grpc.Dial("localhost:9090",
grpc.WithInsecure(), grpc.WithBlock())

 if err != nil {

 log.Fatalf("did not connect: %v", err)

 }

 defer conn.Close()

 c := pb.NewProductServiceClient(conn)


 r, err := c.ListProducts(context.Background(),
&pb.Empty{})

 if err != nil {

 log.Fatalf("could not greet: %v", err)

 }

 log.Printf("Products: %v", r.GetProducts())

}
```

Conclusion

Setting up both REST and gRPC for inter-service communication provides flexibility and performance benefits for microservices architectures. REST is excellent for standard web APIs due to its simplicity and compatibility, while gRPC offers superior performance and is ideal for internal communications between services where low latency and high throughput are critical.

Using gRPC and Protocol Buffers

Introduction to Protocol Buffers and gRPC

Protocol Buffers (Protobuf) and gRPC are technologies developed by Google that are widely used for building efficient, high-performance communication systems. They are particularly popular in microservices architectures for their ability to facilitate robust and fast communication between services.

What are Protocol Buffers?

Protocol Buffers are a language-neutral, platform-neutral, extensible mechanism for serializing structured data, similar to XML, but smaller, faster, and simpler. You define how you want your data to be structured once, then you can use special generated source code to easily write and read your structured data to and from a variety of data streams and using a variety of languages.

Why gRPC?

gRPC is a modern open source high performance Remote Procedure Call (RPC) framework that can run in any environment. It uses HTTP/2 for transport, Protobuf as its interface definition language, and provides features like authentication, load balancing, and more. gRPC is designed to be faster and more efficient than traditional REST APIs because of its binary nature and use of HTTP/2 features like multiplexing to send multiple requests over a single connection.

Service Interfaces and Message Structures with Protocol Buffers

Protocol Buffers allow you to define the structure of the data in a **.proto** file, which is then compiled to generate code in various programming languages. We will create a simple service definition for a hypothetical product service in a microservices architecture.

Install Protocol Buffers Compiler

Before writing any definitions, you need the Protocol Buffers compiler installed:

```
curl -Lo protobuf
```

Define Proto File

Create a file named **product.proto**:

```
syntax = "proto3";


package product;
```

```
// The productService definition.
service ProductService {
 // Sends a greeting
 rpc ListProducts(Empty) returns (ProductResponse);
}

// The request message containing the user's name.
message Empty {}

// The response message containing the greetings
message ProductResponse {
 repeated string products = 1;
}
```

This file defines a **ProductService** with a simple RPC method **ListProducts**, which takes an **Empty** message (no information needed for the request) and returns a **ProductResponse** containing a list of products.

Compile Proto File

Generate the client and server code using the Protobuf compiler:

```
protoc --go_out=. --go_opt=paths=source_relative \
 --go-grpc_out=. --go-grpc_opt=paths=source_relative \
 product.proto
```

The above command generates Go code that includes both the client and server stubs needed to implement and call the gRPC methods defined.

How gRPC utilizes Protocol Buffers?

gRPC uses Protocol Buffers for both defining the service interface and structuring the payload data that will be transported over the network. gRPC leverages HTTP/2's advanced features to create long-lived connections between clients and servers, allowing for a more efficient communication layer that supports bidirectional streaming and flow control out of the box.

Implementing Service

With the generated code, you can implement the **ProductService**:

```
package main


import (
 "context"
 "log"
 "net"

 "google.golang.org/grpc"
 pb "path/to/your/protobuf/package"
)

type server struct {
 pb.UnimplementedProductServiceServer
}
```

```
func (s *server) ListProducts(ctx context.Context, in
*pb.Empty) (*pb.ProductResponse, error) {
 return &pb.ProductResponse{Products: []string{"Apple",
"Banana", "Cherry"}}, nil
}


func main() {
 lis, err := net.Listen("tcp", ":50051")
 if err != nil {
 log.Fatalf("failed to listen: %v", err)
 }
 s := grpc.NewServer()
 pb.RegisterProductServiceServer(s, &server{})
 if err := s.Serve(lis); err != nil {
 log.Fatalf("failed to serve: %v", err)
 }
}
```

In this code snippet, a server is set up to listen on TCP port 50051, and the **ListProducts** method returns a list of products.

Creating the Client

The client setup might look something like this:

```
package main
```

```go
import (
 "context"
 "log"
 "time"

 "google.golang.org/grpc"
 pb "path/to/your/protobuf/package"
)

func main() {
 conn, err := grpc.Dial("localhost:50051",
grpc.WithInsecure(), grpc.WithBlock())
 if err != nil {
 log.Fatalf("did not connect: %v", err)
 }
 defer conn.Close()
 c := pb.NewProductServiceClient(conn)

 ctx, cancel := context.WithTimeout(context.Background(),
time.Second)
 defer cancel()
 r, err := c.ListProducts(ctx, &pb.Empty{})
```

```
    if err != nil {
    log.Fatalf("could not list products: %v", err)
    }
    log.Printf("Products: %v", r.GetProducts())
}
```

This client connects to the gRPC server and calls the **`ListProducts`** method.

By defining data structures and service interfaces in **`.proto`** files, developers can generate boilerplate code for their services and ensure that the contracts between different parts of their system are strictly enforced.

Implementing API Gateways

Introduction to API Gateways

In a microservices architecture, an API Gateway acts as the entry point for all client requests. It routes requests to the appropriate microservice and provides cross-cutting features like authentication, monitoring, and load balancing. By implementing an API Gateway, you can simplify client interactions with your microservices and encapsulate internal architecture changes without affecting the clients.

Significance of an API Gateway

API Gateways play a crucial role in:

- **Routing**: Directs incoming requests to the correct microservice.
- **Aggregation**: Combines data from multiple services and delivers a unified response to the client.
- **Authentication and Authorization**: Ensures that requests are authenticated and authorized before reaching the microservices.
- **Rate Limiting and Quotas**: Protects services from getting overwhelmed by too many requests.
- **Failure Handling**: Manages errors and failures gracefully, ensuring the client receives proper feedback even when services are down.

Implementing an API Gateway

In this demonstration, we will show you how to set up an API Gateway by utilizing Kong, a well-known open-source API Gateway that can be extended through the use of plugins and can be used in conjunction with a service registry such as Consul or directly with specified URLs for services.

Install Kong

First, you need to install Kong, which acts as our API Gateway. Installation instructions vary based on the environment, but Docker can be a simple way to get Kong running quickly:

```
docker run -d --name kong-database \
 -p 5432:5432 \
 -e "POSTGRES_USER=kong" \
 -e "POSTGRES_DB=kong" \
 postgres:9.6

docker run --rm \
 --link kong-database:kong-database \
 -e "KONG_DATABASE=postgres" \
 -e "KONG_PG_HOST=kong-database" \
 kong:latest kong migrations bootstrap

docker run -d --name kong \
 --link kong-database:kong-database \
 -e "KONG_DATABASE=postgres" \
 -e "KONG_PG_HOST=kong-database" \
```

```
-e "KONG_PROXY_ACCESS_LOG=/dev/stdout" \
-e "KONG_ADMIN_ACCESS_LOG=/dev/stdout" \
-e "KONG_PROXY_ERROR_LOG=/dev/stderr" \
-e "KONG_ADMIN_ERROR_LOG=/dev/stderr" \
-e "KONG_ADMIN_LISTEN=0.0.0.0:8001" \
-p 8000:8000 \
-p 8443:8443 \
-p 8001:8001 \
-p 8444:8444 \
kong:latest
```

This sets up Kong with a PostgreSQL database in Docker, runs the necessary database migrations for Kong, and starts the Kong service.

Configure Service Routing

With Kong running, you can add services and set up routes. Assume we have a product service running at **http://localhost:8081/products**. Given below is how to add it to Kong and configure routing:

```
curl -i -X POST \
 --url http://localhost:8001/services/ \
 --data 'name=product-service' \
 --data 'url=http://localhost:8081/products'


curl -i -X POST \
 --url http://localhost:8001/services/product-
```

```
service/routes \
 --data 'hosts[]=gitforgits.com'
```

This setup tells Kong that any request coming to **gitforgits.com** should be routed to the **product-service**.

Handling Failures

To handle failures and ensure high availability, implement health checks and circuit breakers using Kong's plugins, like **circuit-breaker** or **health-checks** plugins, which can be configured as follows:

```
curl -i -X POST \
 --url http://localhost:8001/services/product-
service/plugins/ \
 --data 'name=circuit-breaker' \
 --data 'config.threshold=10' \
 --data 'config.breaker_timeout=300'
```

This configuration adds a circuit breaker to the product service, which will stop forwarding requests to the service if more than 10 failures are detected within 300 seconds, helping prevent cascading failures in **gitforgits.com**.

Implementing Aggregations

For routes that require data from multiple services, Kong can handle aggregations using serverless plugins or by routing requests to an internal service that aggregates data. For instance, a dashboard view might need data from both product and order services:

```
# This is a hypothetical example to demonstrate the
concept
curl -i -X POST \
 --url http://localhost:8001/routes/dashboard-
route/service \
```

```
--data 'name=dashboard-aggregation-service' \
--data 'host=internal-aggregator-service'
```

This above setup with the help of Kong simplifies the complexity of managing multiple microservices.

Authentication and Authorization in Microservices

Introduction to Authentication and Authorization

In a microservices architecture, securing each service from unauthorized access is crucial for maintaining the integrity and confidentiality of the system. Authentication determines if a user is who they claim to be, while authorization determines what an authenticated user is allowed to do. Implementing these controls correctly across a distributed system poses unique challenges due to the decentralized nature of microservices.

Strategies for Securing Microservices

Centralized Identity and Access Management

One common approach to securing microservices is to use a centralized Identity and Access Management (IAM) system. This system handles user authentication and provides tokens (often JWTs) that microservices can use to authorize requests.

Using API Gateways for Security

An API Gateway can act as a control point for authentication and authorization before requests reach individual services. It can validate tokens, enforce security policies, and even handle user sessions, reducing the complexity within each microservice.

Implementing Authentication and Authorization

To demonstrate a basic setup for authentication and authorization across microservices, we continue using Kong for initial authentication and then JWTs for subsequent authorization checks within each service.

Setup Authentication at the API Gateway

Configure the API Gateway to authenticate users and issue JWT tokens. Given below is how you might configure Kong to use its JWT plugin for authentication:

- Enable the JWT Plugin on Kong

```
curl -X POST http://localhost:8001/plugins/ \
 --data "name=jwt" \
 --data "config.claims_to_verify=exp"
```

This above command enables JWT handling on all incoming requests.

- Add a Consumer

```
curl -X POST http://localhost:8001/consumers/ \
 --data "username=user123"
```

- Create a JWT Credential for the Consumer

```
curl -X POST http://localhost:8001/consumers/user123/jwt
\
 -F "algorithm=HS256" \
 -F "key=example_key" \
 -F "secret=example_secret"
```

This creates a JWT credential. The response includes a token that clients can use to authenticate.

Microservice Authorization

Each microservice should independently authorize requests based on the JWT token. Given below is how a service could verify a JWT token using the **github.com/dgrijalva/jwt-go** library:

```
package main


import (
 "fmt"
```

```
"github.com/dgrijalva/jwt-go"

"net/http"

)


func authorize(r *http.Request) error {

tokenString := r.Header.Get("Authorization")

token, err := jwt.Parse(tokenString, func(token
*jwt.Token) (interface{}, error) {

if _, ok := token.Method.(*jwt.SigningMethodHMAC); !ok {

return nil, fmt.Errorf("unexpected signing method")

}

return []byte("example_secret"), nil

})


if err != nil {

return err

}


if claims, ok := token.Claims.(jwt.MapClaims); ok &&
token.Valid {

fmt.Println("User:", claims["user"])

} else {
```

```
return fmt.Errorf("invalid token")
}

return nil
}
```

This function extracts the JWT from the **Authorization** header and validates it. You would call this function in your middleware or handler depending on the framework you are using.

This above demonstrated setup ensures that even if one service is compromised, the damage does not necessarily propagate throughout the entire system.

Containerize Microservices with Kubernetes

Introduction to Kubernetes and Containerization

In the realm of microservices, containerization is a method that encapsulates a microservice and its dependencies into a container that can run consistently across any environment. Kubernetes, also known as K8s, is an open-source system for automating the deployment, scaling, and management of containerized applications.

Setting up Kubernetes

Before diving into containerizing microservices, it's crucial to set up a Kubernetes cluster. For development purposes, Minikube is an excellent choice as it creates a single-node Kubernetes cluster on your local machine.

Install Minikube and kubectl

Minikube is a tool that lets you run Kubernetes locally. Minikube runs a single-node Kubernetes cluster inside a VM on your laptop for users looking to try out Kubernetes or develop with it day-to-day.

```
curl -Lo minikube
https://storage.googleapis.com/minikube/releases/latest/m
inikube-linux-amd64 \

&& chmod +x minikube
```

```
sudo mv minikube /usr/local/bin/
```

kubectl is the Kubernetes command-line tool that allows you to run commands against Kubernetes clusters.

```
curl -LO "https://dl.k8s.io/release/$(curl -L -s
https://dl.k8s.io/release/stable.txt)/bin/linux/amd64/kub
ectl"

chmod +x ./kubectl

sudo mv ./kubectl /usr/local/bin/kubectl
```

Start Minikube

```
minikube start
```

This command starts a local Kubernetes cluster using Minikube. Once started, you can use **kubectl** to interact with your cluster.

Understanding Containerization

Containerization involves packaging software code, its dependencies, system tools, runtime, system libraries, and settings in a container so it can run uniformly and consistently on any infrastructure. Docker is the most popular containerization platform, and it's integral to Kubernetes.

Install Docker

```
curl -fsSL https://get.docker.com -o get-docker.sh

sudo sh get-docker.sh
```

Containerizing Microservices using Gin

We will containerize a simple Gin application. Given below is a basic Gin application that we will containerize:

```
// main.go

package main
```

```
import (
 "github.com/gin-gonic/gin"
 "net/http"
)

func main() {
 r := gin.Default()
 r.GET("/", func(c *gin.Context) {
 c.JSON(http.StatusOK, gin.H{
 "message": "Hello from Gin!",
 })
 })
 r.Run() // listen and serve on 0.0.0.0:8080
}
```

Create a Dockerfile

A Dockerfile is a text document that contains all the commands a user could call on the command line to assemble an image. Given below is a simple Dockerfile for the Gin application:

```
# Use an official Go runtime as a parent image
FROM golang:1.16-alpine

# Set the working directory in the container
```

```
WORKDIR /app

# Copy the current directory contents into the container at /app
COPY . .

# Download all the dependencies
RUN go mod download

# Build the Go app
RUN go build -o main .

# Expose port 8080 to the outside world
EXPOSE 8080

# Command to run the executable
CMD ["./main"]
```

This Dockerfile uses the official Go image, copies your application into the image, installs dependencies, builds your application, and sets the command to run your app.

Build and Run Your Docker Container

- Build your Docker image:

```
docker build -t gin-app .
```

- Run your Docker container:

```
docker run -p 8080:8080 gin-app
```

- The **-p 8080:8080** flag maps port 8080 of the container to port 8080 on your host, allowing you to access the Gin application via **localhost:8080** on your browser or using curl.

Deploying to Kubernetes

- Create a Kubernetes Deployment Configuration: This configuration tells Kubernetes how to create and update instances of your application.

```
# deployment.yaml
apiVersion: apps/v1
kind: Deployment
metadata:
 name: gin-app
spec:
 replicas: 2
 selector:
 matchLabels:
 app: gin-app
 template:
 metadata:
 labels:
 app: gin-app
 spec:
```

```
containers:
- name: gin-app
image: gin-app
ports:
- containerPort: 8080
```

- Create the Deployment on Kubernetes:

```
kubectl apply -f deployment.yaml
```

- Expose the Deployment as a Service:

```
kubectl expose deployment gin-app --type=LoadBalancer --
port=8080
```

The above command creates a service that makes your application accessible via the Minikube load balancer.

This approach encapsulates the application's environment to ensure consistency across development, testing, and production. It also leverages Kubernetes' orchestration capabilities to manage the lifecycle of containers effectively. Containerizing microservices using Docker and deploying them to a Kubernetes cluster using Minikube is a robust strategy for developing scalable, resilient applications.

Summary

In this chapter, we delved deeply into the world of microservices and covered all the bases, covering everything from designing and developing to managing these architectures. Microservices were introduced at the beginning of the chapter with an overview of their design principles, with an emphasis on how services should be built around business capabilities, independently deployable, scalable, and able to handle isolated failure. Following that, we jumped into the technical setup, with a special focus on creating a microservices environment. The Gin framework was covered in it.

Much of this chapter was devoted to learning how services talk to each other; specifically, we looked at how REST and gRPC stack up in microservices designs. We learned that gRPC offers a high-performance, low-latency solution that is perfect for frequent and complicated interactions between services, whereas REST is more suited to simpler, less frequent communications over HTTP.

Following that, API Gateways were defined, and their ability to process requests, direct them to the right services, and deal with errors was exhibited. Also learned were methods for authenticating and authorizing users to access microservices securely. We looked at how token-based authorization and centralized identity management can prevent unauthorized access to services and keep data intact. Kubernetes containerization of microservices was the last topic covered in the chapter. By learning how to use Kubernetes to manage service containers, we were able to automate the deployment, scaling, and management of containerized applications.

Chapter 7: Message Brokering with NSQ and Apache Kafka

Chapter Overview

Focusing on the integration and utilization of NSQ and Apache Kafka, this chapter delves into the vital topic of message brokering within software architectures. With these tools, applications can handle messages more efficiently, which improves their communication, scalability, and resilience.

To begin, there is an introductory section on message brokering that defines the term and teaches its relevance to modern distributed systems. In this section, we will go over the basics of message brokers and how they help with asynchronous communication in systems, which in turn improves scalability and modularity by separating services. The next topic will be NSQ Application Setup. When it comes to distributed environments, NSQ is your best bet for a lightweight, highly available messaging platform. In this section, we will show you how to configure and deploy NSQ so that your application can handle message traffic efficiently. After NSQ, we will go on to the next topic, which is integrating Apache Kafka with Go. One powerful open-source platform for stream processing is Apache Kafka, which can process trillions of events daily. Creating Kafka clusters and writing Go apps that send and receive messages through Kafka are two of the many practical components of integrating Kafka with Go applications that we will go through. Common messaging patterns like publish/subscribe and message queues will be covered in section 'Handling Message Patterns'. In it, we will go over the implementation of these patterns in NSQ and Kafka.

The chapter then dives into the process of designing systems that guarantee message delivery in the event of failures. Last but not least, the section 'Scaling and Managing Brokers' looks into tactics for efficiently managing and scaling message brokering systems in response to increasing demand. Both NSQ and Kafka performance tuning tips, monitoring practices, and scaling techniques will be covered in this chapter.

Introduction to Message Brokering

Concept of Message Brokering

Message brokering is a critical architectural technique used in distributed systems to manage the communication or exchange of information between different applications and services without having them interact with each other directly. This approach is fundamental in modern application architecture, especially in environments characterized by high scalability, reliability, and modularity demands.

What is a Message Broker?

A message broker is a software system that enables applications, systems, and services to communicate with each other by sending messages (data) through a virtual channel. This intermediary service ensures that messages are delivered from one program (the producer) to another (the consumer), possibly through various processing rules that include routing, translating, and transforming the data as required.

Following are the core functions of the message brokers:

- **Routing**: Message brokers route messages between services based on specific rules and logic defined within the broker or the architecture. This routing can be simple (point-to-point) or complex (topic-based or content-based routing).
- **Transformation**: They can transform messages to the appropriate formats required by the consumer service, ensuring compatibility across different systems and services within the architecture.
- **Mediation**: Brokers can handle the invocation of business logic processing, integrating legacy systems and various back-ends without changing the systems themselves.
- **Asynchronous Communication**: This is perhaps the most critical function, where message brokers allow communication between services without requiring the parties to interact with the message simultaneously.

Benefits of Asynchronous Communication

Asynchronous communication means that the sender and the receiver do not need to interact with the message at the same time. The message broker keeps the message until the receiver is ready to process it, allowing both parties to operate independently. This method contrasts with synchronous communication, where the sender must wait for the receiver to acknowledge receipt of the message before continuing its process, which can lead to bottlenecks and inefficiencies.

Following are the benefits of the asynchronous communication:

- **Decoupling**: Producers and consumers are decoupled both temporally (do not need to operate at the same time) and spatially (do not need to know each other's network locations). This separation enhances the flexibility and scalability of applications and services.
- **Reliability**: Message brokers can enhance reliability through durable messaging that ensures messages are not lost, even if the receiving service is temporarily unavailable. The broker can store messages and retry sending them until they are successfully processed.
- **Scalability**: Asynchronous systems can handle higher loads by adding more consumers without affecting the producer's performance or increasing the response time.
- **Flexibility**: New services can be added or modified without disrupting existing services. This flexibility facilitates smoother and incremental updates and changes within the system.

Message brokers are widely used across different industries and scenarios. Following are a few practical examples:

1. **E-Commerce Applications**: Brokers manage orders, inventory updates, and customer notifications without coupling the front-end and inventory management systems directly.
2. **Financial Services**: In trading platforms, brokers facilitate the flow of trade orders and transactions across multiple financial institutions without direct connections between these entities.
3. **IoT Applications**: In IoT architectures, brokers can manage messages from millions of devices, processing them to update databases and trigger actions without direct links between devices and processing systems.
4. **Logistics and Supply Chain Management**: Brokers handle updates across various checkpoints in a supply chain, updating systems asynchronously as goods move from one point to another.

Modern, efficient, and resilient application development relies heavily on the idea of message brokering. Message brokers improve system scalability, flexibility, and reliability by enabling asynchronous communication. The architecture is simplified and dependencies are reduced because they allow different parts of a system to communicate effectively without being directly connected.

Setting up NSQ

NSQ is a real-time distributed messaging platform designed to operate at scale, handling billions of messages per day. It is built to decentralized topologies without a single point of failure, maximizing fault tolerance and reliability while maintaining simplicity and ease of deployment. NSQ is known for its performance and flexibility in routing messages based on topics and channels without complex setup procedures.

Key Features of NSQ

- NSQ is easy to configure and deploy, requiring minimal setup. It's designed to be high performance and can handle thousands of messages per second per instance.
- It supports distributed operation out-of-the-box, meaning it can run across multiple nodes, which is ideal for fault tolerance and high availability.
- NSQ operates without relying on a central broker (masterless), which means that each node is independent, and there is no single point of failure in the system.
- NSQ comes with nsqadmin, a built-in web UI that helps you monitor and manage your NSQ instances and topics.

Setting up NSQ in Development Environment

Installing and setting up NSQ involves setting up **nsqd**, which is the daemon that receives, queues, and delivers messages to clients, **nsqlookupd**, which is the daemon providing discovery services to **nsqd** instances, and **nsqadmin**, the web UI for monitoring cluster state.

Install NSQ

NSQ binaries are available for various platforms. You can download them directly or pull them using **go get**. Given below is how to install NSQ:

```
go get -u github.com/nsqio/nsq
```

Alternatively, you can download pre-built binaries for your platform from the NSQ releases page.

Run 'nsqlookupd'

nsqlookupd is the service discovery daemon that manages topology information. To start **nsqlookupd**, run:

```
nsqlookupd
```

This command will start **nsqlookupd** listening on the default ports (TCP port 4160 and HTTP port 4161).

Run 'nsqd'

nsqd is the daemon that handles the queueing of messages. It needs to know how to communicate with **nsqlookupd**. Start **nsqd** with the address of **nsqlookupd**:

```
nsqd --lookupd-tcp-address=localhost:4160
```

This tells **nsqd** to register with **nsqlookupd** at **localhost** on port **4160**. **nsqd** listens on the default TCP port 4150 for clients and HTTP port 4151 for HTTP requests.

Run 'nsqadmin'

nsqadmin is a Web UI to view and administer the NSQ cluster. Start **nsqadmin** and point it to **nsqlookupd**:

```
nsqadmin --lookupd-http-address=localhost:4161
```

This will start **nsqadmin** which you can access by visiting **http://localhost:4171/** in your browser. Here, you can see real-time statistics and perform various administrative tasks.

Testing NSQ Setup

To test if NSQ is set up correctly, you can publish a message to a topic using **curl** and then consume it using another tool or custom client:

- Publish a Message:

```
curl -d 'hello world'
'http://127.0.0.1:4151/pub?topic=test'
```

This command sends a message "hello world" to the **test** topic.

- Consume the Message:

You can write a simple consumer or use **nsq_tail** to print messages to the console:

```
nsq_tail --topic=test --lookupd-http-
address=localhost:4161
```

The design of NSQ promotes scalable and resilient message brokering through the use of a decentralized system that gracefully handles failures. Applications can decouple components, scale operations, and improve overall reliability and performance with this setup by effectively leveraging message queuing.

Integrating Apache Kafka with Go

Apache Kafka is a distributed streaming platform capable of handling trillions of events a day. Initially conceived as a messaging queue, Kafka is based on an abstraction of a distributed commit log. Since its inception, it has developed into a full-fledged event streaming platform capable of not just publishing and subscribing to streams of records but also storing and processing them as they occur.

Installing Apache Kafka

To integrate Kafka with a Go application, you first need to install and run Kafka, which depends on ZooKeeper for cluster management. Given below is how you can set up Kafka locally for development purposes:

- Go to the Apache Kafka website and download the latest binary files.
- Extract the files:

```
tar -xzf kafka_2.13-2.7.0.tgz

cd kafka_2.13-2.7.0
```

- Start ZooKeeper:

```
bin/zookeeper-server-start.sh config/zookeeper.properties
```

ZooKeeper starts on default port 2181. ZooKeeper is necessary for managing Kafka's cluster state and configurations.

- Start Kafka:

```
bin/kafka-server-start.sh config/server.properties
```

Kafka runs on default port 9092. With Kafka running, you can now integrate it into your Go applications.

Integrating Kafka with Go

To integrate Kafka with Go, you need a Kafka client library. **confluent-kafka-go** is one of the most popular Kafka Go client libraries, providing both producer and consumer functionalities based on **librdkafka**.

Install Kafka Go Client Library

Install **confluent-kafka-go**:

```
go get -u github.com/confluentinc/confluent-kafka-
go/kafka
```

Writing a Kafka Producer

A Kafka producer sends messages to Kafka topics. Given below is how you can implement a basic Kafka producer:

```
package main


import (
```

```
"fmt"
"github.com/confluentinc/confluent-kafka-go/kafka"
)

func main() {
producer, err :=
kafka.NewProducer(&kafka.ConfigMap{"bootstrap.servers":
"localhost:9092"})
if err != nil {
panic(err)
}
defer producer.Close()

// Delivery report handler for produced messages
go func() {
for e := range producer.Events() {
switch ev := e.(type) {
case *kafka.Message:
if ev.TopicPartition.Error != nil {
fmt.Printf("Failed to deliver message: %v\n",
ev.TopicPartition.Error)
} else {
```

```
 fmt.Printf("Successfully produced record to topic %s
partition [%d] @ offset %v\n",
 *ev.TopicPartition.Topic, ev.TopicPartition.Partition,
ev.TopicPartition.Offset)
 }
 }
 }
 }()

 topic := "test"
 for _, word := range []string{"Welcome", "to", "Kafka"}
{
 producer.Produce(&kafka.Message{
 TopicPartition: kafka.TopicPartition{Topic: &topic,
Partition: kafka.PartitionAny},
 Value: []byte(word),
 }, nil)
 }

 // Wait for message deliveries before shutting down
 producer.Flush(15 * 1000)
}
```

This producer sends three messages to the **test** topic.

Writing a Kafka Consumer

A Kafka consumer reads messages from Kafka topics. Given below is a basic consumer:

```
package main

import (
 "fmt"
 "github.com/confluentinc/confluent-kafka-go/kafka"
)

func main() {
 consumer, err := kafka.NewConsumer(&kafka.ConfigMap{
 "bootstrap.servers": "localhost:9092",
 "group.id": "myGroup",
 "auto.offset.reset": "earliest",
 })

 if err != nil {
 panic(err)
 }

 consumer.SubscribeTopics([]string{"test"}, nil)
```

```
for {
msg, err := consumer.ReadMessage(-1)
if err == nil {
fmt.Printf("Message on %s: %s\n", msg.TopicPartition,
string(msg.Value))
} else {
fmt.Printf("Consumer error: %v (%v)\n", err, msg)
break
}
}

consumer.Close()
}
```

This consumer subscribes to the **`test`** topic and prints out each message it receives. By utilizing Kafka's capabilities to manage reliable and high-throughput message streaming, this configuration enables Go applications to efficiently generate and consume messages.

Handling Message Patterns

Messaging patterns are foundational to effective communication and data flow within distributed systems like microservices. Two of the most prevalent patterns are publish/subscribe (pub/sub) and queues. Each serves distinct purposes, facilitates scalability, and enhances system resilience.

Understanding Pub/Sub and Queues

- **Publish/Subscribe (Pub/Sub)**: In this pattern, messages are published to a "topic" rather than directly to a single consumer. Any number of subscribers can listen to or subscribe to this topic and receive messages when they are published. This pattern is useful for broadcasting data, such as real-time status updates or event notifications, to multiple interested consumers simultaneously.

- **Queues**: This pattern ensures that a message is processed by exactly one consumer. Messages are sent to a queue and processed by a single consumer in a First In, First Out (FIFO) manner. It is ideal for tasks that need to be processed in order or where each task is only processed once, such as processing a bank transaction or an order in an e-commerce platform.

Implementing Pub/Sub and Queues

We will integrate Apache Kafka for Pub/Sub and NSQ for queues into a basic service architecture that handles new user registrations and notifications to show these patterns.

Implementing Pub/Sub with Kafka

Think of a situation wherein, when a new user registers, multiple parts of the application need to react, such as the email service sending a welcome email and the analytics service updating statistics.

- First, create a topic for registration events:

```
kafka-topics --create --topic user-registrations --
bootstrap-server localhost:9092 --partitions 3 --
replication-factor 1
```

- A simple producer sends a message to the **`user-registrations`** topic whenever a new user registers.

```
package main


import (
 "context"
 "github.com/segmentio/kafka-go"
 "log"
)
```

```go
func main() {
 w := &kafka.Writer{
 Addr: kafka.TCP("localhost:9092"),
 Topic: "user-registrations",
 Balancer: &kafka.LeastBytes{},
 }

 err := w.WriteMessages(context.Background(),
 kafka.Message{
 Value: []byte("New user registered"),
 },
 )
 if err != nil {
 log.Fatalf("failed to write messages: %s", err)
 }

 if err := w.Close(); err != nil {
 log.Fatalf("failed to close writer: %s", err)
 }
}
```

- Services that need to react to the registration implement consumers that subscribe to the **`user-registrations`** topic.

```
package main

import (
 "context"
 "fmt"
 "github.com/segmentio/kafka-go"
)

func main() {
 r := kafka.NewReader(kafka.ReaderConfig{
 Brokers: []string{"localhost:9092"},
 Topic: "user-registrations",
 GroupID: "email-service",
 })
 for {
 msg, err := r.ReadMessage(context.Background())
 if err != nil {
 break
 }
 fmt.Printf("received: %s\n", string(msg.Value))
 // Process the message
```

```
 }
 if err := r.Close(); err != nil {
 fmt.Printf("failed to close reader: %s", err)
 }
}
```

Implementing Queues with NSQ

To understand this better, consider a scenario wherein you have to process user feedback messages one at a time to ensure each message is dealt with sequentially and without loss.

- Assuming NSQ is running, you would write to a specific topic as users submit feedback.

```
package main


import (
 "github.com/nsqio/go-nsq"
 "log"
)


func main() {
 config := nsq.NewConfig()
 producer, err := nsq.NewProducer("localhost:4150",
config)
 if err != nil {
 log.Fatal(err)
```

```
}

err = producer.Publish("feedback", []byte("User feedback received"))
if err != nil {
log.Fatal("Could not publish message: ", err)
}

producer.Stop()
}
```

- Processing Messages from the Queue:

```
package main

import (
"github.com/nsqio/go-nsq"
"log"
)

func main() {
config := nsq.NewConfig()
consumer, err := nsq.NewConsumer("feedback", "default", config)
```

```
if err != nil {
log.Fatal(err)
}

consumer.AddHandler(nsq.HandlerFunc(func(message
*nsq.Message) error {
log.Printf("Got a message: %v", string(message.Body))
return nil
}))

err = consumer.ConnectToNSQD("localhost:4150")
if err != nil {
log.Fatal("Could not connect to queue: ", err)
}

<-consumer.StopChan
}
```

Events impacting numerous system components at once are well-suited to Kafka's pub/sub model, which enables extensive data distribution. By contrast, the order and integrity of critical operations are preserved by NSQ's queue model, which guarantees the reliable handling of tasks requiring singular processing without loss or duplication.

Ensuring Message Delivery and System

Resilience

In an asynchronous system utilizing message brokers like NSQ and Kafka, ensuring that messages are consistently delivered and the system remains resilient in the face of faults is crucial. This involves implementing strategies that address potential points of failure and efficiently managing message flows to prevent data loss.

Key Concepts

Message Delivery Guarantees

- **At-most-once**: Ensures that messages are delivered no more than once, but some messages may be lost.
- **At-least-once**: Guarantees that messages are delivered at least once, potentially causing duplicates.
- **Exactly-once**: Ensures each message is delivered exactly once, which is the hardest to achieve and often requires complex coordination between the producer, broker, and consumer.

System Resilience

- **Fault Tolerance**: The system's ability to continue operating properly in the event of a failure of some of its components.
- **High Availability**: Ensuring the system or service is continuously operational for a desirably long length of time.

Implementation Strategies

Scenario 1: Ensuring At-Least-Once Delivery in Kafka

Kafka inherently supports at-least-once delivery, but it must be correctly configured. Following is how you can achieve it:

- Producer Configuration:

Ensure that the producer receives acknowledgments from the broker to confirm message writes:

```
producer, err := kafka.NewProducer(&kafka.ConfigMap{
 "bootstrap.servers": "localhost:9092",
 "acks": "all", // Ensure all replicas acknowledge
```

```
 "enable.idempotence": true, // Prevents data duplication
})
```

This configuration ensures that the Kafka producer does not consider a message as successfully sent until all in-sync replicas have acknowledged its receipt. Enabling idempotence prevents the producer from sending duplicates in case of network errors.

- Consumer Configuration:

Make sure the consumer manages offsets properly to avoid message loss:

```
consumer, err := kafka.NewConsumer(&kafka.ConfigMap{
 "bootstrap.servers": "localhost:9092",
 "group.id": "myGroup",
 "auto.offset.reset": "earliest",
 "enable.auto.commit": false,
})
```

Manually managing the offsets and disabling auto-commit allows the consumer to control when a message is considered 'processed' by committing the offset. This way, if a consumer fails before committing, it will restart from the last committed offset.

Scenario 2: Handling Failures and Redundancies in NSQ

For NSQ, which does not guarantee message durability on its own, you need to implement additional mechanisms:

- Message Redelivery:

If a message processing fails, NSQ requeues the message automatically, provided the message timeout hasn't expired:

```
consumer.AddHandler(nsq.HandlerFunc(func(message
*nsq.Message) error {
 if err := processMessage(message); err != nil {
 message.Requeue(-1) // Requeue immediately
```

```
return nil

}

return nil

}))
```

In the above script, if **processMessage** fails, the message is requeued for another attempt.

- High Availability Setup:

Deploy NSQ in a highly available configuration with multiple instances of **nsqd** and **nsqlookupd** across different machines or zones to provide redundancy.

Reliable and robust operation of asynchronous messaging systems relies on handling message redelivery in NSQ and ensuring at-least-once delivery in Kafka. For systems that must be highly available and reliable in production settings, these measures are essential, even though they increase system complexity.

Scaling and Managing Brokers

In distributed systems, the ability to scale out (horizontal scaling) is essential for handling increased load and ensuring high availability. NSQ and Kafka, both being high-performance message brokers, provide mechanisms to scale horizontally but in slightly different ways due to their underlying architectures.

Scaling NSQ

NSQ is designed to be a lightweight message broker with decentralized features that naturally support horizontal scaling. Scaling NSQ involves adding more instances of **nsqd**, the daemon responsible for receiving, queueing, and delivering messages to clients.

The fundamental scaling unit in NSQ is an **nsqd** instance. Each **nsqd** operates independently, which simplifies scaling:

- You can start additional **nsqd** instances on new machines or containers. Each instance should be configured to communicate with the same set of **nsqlookupd** services to maintain service discovery integrity. Following is the sample command to start an **nsqd** instance:

```
nsqd --lookupd-tcp-address=existing-nsqlookupd-host:4160
```

- Although **nsqd** instances are independent, you should implement a load-balancing mechanism to distribute the producer load evenly across multiple **nsqd** nodes. This can be done at the application level, where the application logic includes algorithms to distribute messages across available **nsqd** instances based on certain criteria like least connections or round-robin.
- Scaling out requires robust monitoring to ensure that each node performs optimally and does not become a bottleneck. NSQ provides stats accessible via HTTP on each node that can be integrated with monitoring tools to track performance and issues.

Scaling Kafka Horizontally

To improve parallelism and throughput, Kafka uses partitioning mechanisms to distribute data across a cluster of brokers, allowing it to scale. Kafka allows for the splitting of topics into multiple partitions, and then distributes these partitions among numerous brokers.

Adding More Brokers

You can scale Kafka by adding more brokers to your Kafka cluster. Adding brokers increases the capacity of the cluster to handle more messages. Following are the steps to add a broker:

- Provision a new server with adequate resources.
- Install Kafka.
- Configure the new broker with the correct **broker.id** and ensure it points to the same ZooKeeper cluster.
- Start the new Kafka broker.

Partition Rebalancing

Simply adding brokers doesn't automatically lead to increased performance unless topics are configured to utilize these additional brokers. You may need to increase the number of partitions for existing topics and then reassign these partitions across the new set of brokers. For example, use the Kafka tooling to add partitions:

```
kafka-topics --alter --zookeeper zk-host:port --topic
your-topic --partitions 20
```

This above command increases the number of partitions for **your-topic**. After increasing partitions, use the partition reassignment tool in Kafka to distribute these partitions across the new brokers.

Replication Factor

When scaling out, also consider the replication factor of your topics. A higher replication factor can improve fault tolerance but at the cost of higher disk space and network traffic. Ensure your system is configured to handle these additional resources.

Monitoring and Managing Performance

As you scale out, monitoring becomes critical. Kafka provides JMX metrics that can be used with monitoring tools to track the performance of each broker in the cluster. Monitor parameters like CPU usage, memory usage, disk I/O, and network I/O.

Summary

This chapter explored the complex nature of message brokering, specifically looking at two strong tools that help distributed systems communicate efficiently: NSQ and Apache Kafka. An overview of message brokering was provided at the beginning of the chapter, along with an explanation of its role in facilitating asynchronous communication—a prerequisite for decoupling different components of a system. After that, the chapter went on to explain how to set up NSQ, and how to integrate it into an existing development environment. The chapter then demonstrated the practical use of NSQ in real-time data handling and fault tolerance by teaching you how to configure it to handle messages effectively. On the other hand, we also learned to integrate Apache Kafka with Go, which shows how well Kafka handles processing messages on a large scale. Horizontal scaling of NSQ and Kafka was also emphasized as a key technique for managing brokers and scaling up to handle increased loads while maintaining high availability.

At the chapter's conclusion, you will have solid knowledge on the ins and outs of NSQ and Kafka-based message brokering solutions, with the knowledge to build and oversee these solutions with confidence, allowing your applications to scale with ease while keeping performance and reliability at a premium.

CHAPTER 8: SECURING GO APPLICATIONS

Chapter Overview

Protecting Go applications from common vulnerabilities is the primary goal of this chapter, which covers both the fundamental coding practices and the specific security implementations. At the outset of the chapter, we cover secure coding practices, which include making sure your code works as intended while also safeguarding it from possible security breaches. This involves doing things the right way to prevent typical mistakes that could cause security issues. Following this, we will explore the details of utilizing Go's crypto/tls package for HTTPS. Protecting sensitive data while it is in transit is essential, and this section explains how to configure and set up TLS/SSL protocols to accomplish just that.

Securing headers and cookies is the next topic covered in the chapter. These are two of the most important ways to ensure that sensitive information transmitted between a client and server remains intact and private. The methods for preventing attacks such as request forgery and cross-site scripting (XSS) are thoroughly taught, along with how to set secure headers and cookie attributes. This chapter also covers how to prevent cross-site scripting (XSS) and SQL injections. The chapter continues by explaining how to protect Go apps from these common threats to data privacy and integrity. As an example of secure user authentication and authorization, we go further into the use of OAuth2 and JWT to provide secure data access. Tokens must be handled efficiently and securely so that resources can be controlled without putting them at risk.

Finally, auditing and security testing are covered in the chapter's end. In order to make sure that Go applications are secure and can adapt to new threats as they come up, it describes ways to test and review them in a systematic way.

Secure Coding Practices

Source Code and Binaries Checks

Secure coding practices are essential to protect applications from vulnerabilities and attacks. For Go, these practices encompass a range of techniques from source code checks to the use of built-in tools like Go's **vet** command, race detection, and more.

Source Code Analysis

Analyzing the source code for potential security flaws is a crucial first step. Static analysis tools can help identify common programming errors that might lead to security vulnerabilities. For Go, tools like **Go Meta Linter** or **Staticcheck** provide comprehensive checks that go beyond the standard linting tools to analyze code for bugs that could potentially be exploited.

Following is the quick installation of Staticcheck:

```
go get -u honnef.co/go/tools/cmd/staticcheck
```

```
iccheck ./...
```

This tool runs a series of checks on your Go code to find bugs, unused code, and possible optimizations.

Binaries Analysis

After compiling your applications, it's important to analyze the binaries to ensure that there are no embedded vulnerabilities or unexpected behaviors. Tools like **`gobinaryanalysis`** and **`GoSafe`** can scan Go binaries for various security issues, providing an extra layer of assurance.

Updating Dependencies and Go

Regularly updating the dependencies and the Go compiler itself is critical to securing your applications. Each new release of Go and its libraries can include security patches along with performance improvements and bug fixes. For instance, if you want to check for outdated packages:

```
go get -u github.com/psampaz/go-mod-outdated

go list -u -m -json all | go-mod-outdated -update -direct
```

This above command helps identify outdated direct dependencies, allowing you to update them systematically.

Fuzz Testing

Fuzz testing is an advanced technique used to test applications by inputting massive amounts of random data ("fuzz") to the program in an attempt to make it crash. Fuzz testing can uncover unexpected flaws in your logic that could be exploited maliciously.

Go 1.18+ includes support for native fuzz testing. To add a fuzz test:

```
// +build gofuzz



package yourpkg



import "testing"
```

```
func FuzzYourFunction(f *testing.F) {
 f.Add("initial") // Initial input
 f.Fuzz(func(t *testing.T, in string) {
 YourFunction(in)
 })
}
```

Run the fuzz test using:

```
go test -fuzz=Fuzz
```

Race Detection

Concurrency can lead to race conditions, which might not only cause crashes or unpredictable behavior but also lead to security vulnerabilities.

Detect race conditions by:

```
go test -race ./...
```

This command will help detect race conditions in your code, signaling where you might need to add locks or rethink your concurrency model.

Using Go's Vet Command

The **go vet** command examines Go source code and reports suspicious constructs, such as Printf calls whose arguments do not align with the format string. It can catch subtle bugs in code that might otherwise go unnoticed.

Run Go vet:

```
go vet ./...
```

This is good practice to integrate into your CI/CD pipeline to catch issues early.

With these secure coding practices in place, Go applications are much more secure and reliable.

This is because developers routinely update their code, test it thoroughly, and implement proactive security measures to keep software secure in the face of constantly changing cyber threats.

Using HTTPS with Crypto/TLS

Transport Layer Security (TLS) is the foundation for securing communications over the internet, providing confidentiality, integrity, and authentication between two parties. In Go, the **crypto/tls** package offers comprehensive functionalities for managing TLS-enabled connections. Using HTTPS (HTTP Secure) ensures that communications between clients and servers are encrypted, safeguarding data against eavesdropping and tampering.

Understanding crypto/tls Package

The **crypto/tls** package implements the TLS protocol, which is used primarily for protected communication over the web. This package allows developers to configure servers and clients with required security parameters, such as certificates, cipher suites, and TLS versions, providing a robust mechanism to handle secure connections.

Setting up HTTPS Server with TLS

To set up an HTTPS server, you need to generate TLS certificates, configure the server to use these certificates, and then handle requests securely. Following is how to implement this:

Generate TLS Certificates

For development purposes, you can generate self-signed certificates using OpenSSL. For production, you should obtain certificates from a trusted Certificate Authority (CA).

```
openssl req -x509 -newkey rsa:4096 -keyout key.pem -out
cert.pem -days 365 -nodes
```

The above command generates a new private key (**key.pem**) and a self-signed certificate (**cert.pem**) valid for 365 days.

Configure HTTPS Server

Once you have your certificates, you can configure an HTTPS server as follows:

```
package main
```

```
import (
 "crypto/tls"
 "log"
 "net/http"
)

func handler(w http.ResponseWriter, r *http.Request) {
 w.Header().Set("Content-Type", "text/plain")
 w.Write([]byte("This is an example server.\n"))
}

func main() {
 http.HandleFunc("/", handler)

 // Configure TLS settings
 cfg := &tls.Config{
 MinVersion: tls.VersionTLS12, // Specify the TLS version
to enhance security
 PreferServerCipherSuites: true, // Use the server's
preference of cipher suites
 CurvePreferences: []tls.CurveID{tls.CurveP256,
tls.X25519}, // Specify elliptic curves
```

```
}

srv := &http.Server{
Addr: ":443",
Handler: nil,
TLSConfig: cfg,
TLSNextProto: make(map[string]func(*http.Server,
*tls.Conn, http.Handler), 0), // Disable HTTP/2
}

// Serve using TLS
log.Fatal(srv.ListenAndServeTLS("cert.pem", "key.pem"))
}
```

In the above sample program, an HTTP server is set up that listens on port 443 (standard port for HTTPS). The server uses TLS configurations specified in the **`tls.Config`** struct to ensure the use of modern security settings.

Test HTTPS Server

You can test the server by accessing **`https://localhost`** or using a tool like **`curl`**:

```
curl -k https://localhost
```

The **`-k`** flag tells **`curl`** to ignore certificate warnings, which you'll see with self-signed certificates. While doing so, ensure the following enhancement and security considerations:

- **HTTP Strict Transport Security (HSTS)**: Add HSTS headers to your responses to enforce secure connections on compliant browsers.
- **Certificate Pinning**: Implement certificate pinning in your client applications to mitigate the risk of man-in-the-middle (MITM) attacks.

- **Logging and Monitoring**: Implement logging and monitoring to detect unusual patterns that might indicate a security breach or a configuration issue.

For applications to function in regulated environments or with sensitive data, the above mentioned configuration is essential. By adhering to these standards, programmers can make their Go apps resistant to typical network attacks.

Securing Headers and Cookies

To prevent web security vulnerabilities like session hijacking, Cross-Site Request Forgery (CSRF), and Cross-Site Scripting (XSS), it is essential to secure HTTP headers and cookies. This will protect the application and its users. Here you'll learn the best practices for securing headers and cookies to lessen the impact of these threats.

Configuring HTTP Headers Securely

HTTP headers allow the client and the server to pass additional information with an HTTP request or response. Headers can control behavior in browsers, instructing them on how to handle content or manage security features.

Content-Security-Policy (CSP)

The Content-Security-Policy header helps prevent XSS attacks by restricting the resources the browser is allowed to load for a page. For example, you can specify which scripts, styles, or images are legitimate, reducing the risk of malicious content execution.

```
w.Header().Set("Content-Security-Policy", "default-src
'self'; script-src 'self' https://apis.gitforgits.com")
```

This policy allows scripts from the site's own domain and APIs from 'https://apis.gitforgits.com', but nowhere else.

X-Content-Type-Options

This header prevents the browser from interpreting files as something else than declared by the content type in the HTTP headers.

```
w.Header().Set("X-Content-Type-Options", "nosniff")
```

It stops the browser from MIME-sniffing a response away from the declared content-type.

X-Frame-Options

X-Frame-Options can prevent your content from being framed (used within **<iframe>**, **<object>**, etc.), which can protect against clickjacking attacks.

```
w.Header().Set("X-Frame-Options", "DENY")
```

This setting denies all framing attempts, regardless of origin.

Strict-Transport-Security

The HTTP Strict Transport Security (HSTS) header ensures that browsers only use secure (HTTPS) connections to the server. This header can only be set over HTTPS connections.

```
w.Header().Set("Strict-Transport-Security", "max-
age=63072000; includeSubDomains")
```

This policy declares that browsers should remember to access the site using HTTPS for the next two years, including all subdomains.

Securely Configuring Cookies

Cookies frequently hold private session information. Protecting session integrity, particularly against interception via man-in-the-middle (MITM) attacks, requires securing cookies.

- HttpOnly

The **HttpOnly** flag makes the cookie inaccessible to client-side scripts, reducing risks of XSS attacks.

```
http.SetCookie(w, &http.Cookie{

 Name: "sessionId",

 Value: sessionToken,

 HttpOnly: true,

 Path: "/",

 Secure: true,

})
```

This cookie can't be accessed by JavaScript, which helps prevent XSS attacks.

- Secure

The **Secure** flag ensures that cookies are only sent over secure HTTPS connections.

```
http.Cookie{
 Secure: true,
}
```

This setting prevents the cookie from being sent over an insecure HTTP connection, mitigating the risk of MITM attacks.

- SameSite

The **SameSite** cookie attribute helps mitigate CSRF attacks by instructing the browser not to send the cookie with cross-site requests.

```
http.Cookie{
 SameSite: http.SameSiteStrictMode,
}
```

SameSite=Strict ensures the cookie is only sent in a first-party context, providing the highest level of protection against CSRF.

Sample Program: Configuring Headers and Cookies

When developing Go web applications, these headers and cookie settings should be implemented consistently across all responses. Middleware is an effective way to ensure that every HTTP response includes the necessary security headers and that cookies are set with the correct flags. Following is a quick sample program:

```
func secureHeaders(next http.Handler) http.Handler {
 return http.HandlerFunc(func(w http.ResponseWriter, r
*http.Request) {
 w.Header().Set("Strict-Transport-Security", "max-
age=63072000; includeSubDomains")
 w.Header().Set("X-Frame-Options", "DENY")
```

```
 w.Header().Set("X-Content-Type-Options", "nosniff")

 w.Header().Set("Content-Security-Policy", "default-src
'self'")

 next.ServeHTTP(w, r)

 })

}
```

Developers can significantly improve the security of their Go applications by carefully configuring both HTTP headers and cookies. Any secure deployment of a web application must include these settings, as they help prevent a number of common web vulnerabilities.

Preventing SQL Injections and XSS Attacks

Some of the most prevalent and harmful web security vulnerabilities include SQL Injection and Cross-Site Scripting (XSS). In order to steal data, hijack user sessions, or deface websites, these attacks take advantage of security weaknesses in web applications. When it comes to protecting web applications, knowing these attacks and how to prevent them is top priority.

Prevent SQL Injections

SQL Injection occurs when an attacker inserts or injects a SQL query via the input data from the client to the application. A successful SQL injection exploit can read sensitive data from the database, modify database data (Insert/Update/Delete), execute administration operations on the database (such as shutdown the DBMS), and in some cases, issue commands to the operating system.

Following are some of the preventive techniques:

Use Prepared Statements (Parameterized Queries)

The most effective way to prevent SQL injection attacks is to use prepared statements with parameterized queries. These statements ensure that an attacker cannot change the intent of a query, even if SQL commands are inserted by an attacker. In Go, you can use prepared statements with the standard **database/sql** package:

```
db, err := sql.Open("postgres", "connection_string_here")

if err != nil {
```

```
    log.Fatal(err)
}
defer db.Close()

stmt, err := db.Prepare("INSERT INTO users (username, password) VALUES ($1, $2)")
if err != nil {
    log.Fatal(err)
}
defer stmt.Close()

_, err = stmt.Exec("newuser", "newpassword")
if err != nil {
    log.Fatal(err)
}
```

Escaping All User Inputs

Although less recommended than parameterized queries, escaping user inputs can also help prevent SQL injections. Escaping involves making the input safe before including it in a SQL query.

Prevent XSS Attacks

Cross-Site Scripting (XSS) occurs when an attacker injects malicious scripts into content from a trusted website. This script then runs in the browser of any user who views the malicious content. These scripts can steal cookies, change page content, or redirect the user to another page.

Following are some of the preventive techniques:

Encoding and Escaping User Input

Encoding user input converts potentially dangerous characters into a safe encoded representation. Go provides several packages that can help encode data:

```
import "html/template"


func handler(w http.ResponseWriter, r *http.Request) {

 tmpl :=
template.Must(template.New("example").Parse("<h1>{{.}}</h
1>"))

 tmpl.Execute(w, r.FormValue("user_input"))

}
```

The above code snippet uses Go's **`html/template`** package which automatically escapes inputs when rendering HTML which can help prevent XSS.

Use Content Security Policy (CSP)

A Content Security Policy can significantly reduce the severity of XSS attacks by restricting the sources from which content can be loaded or executed. It can be declared via HTTP headers:

```
w.Header().Set("Content-Security-Policy", "default-src
'self'; script-src 'self'")
```

Apart from the above two, do not trust any user input, rather validate the input to ensure it conforms to expected parameters (e.g., using regular expressions). Sanitization libraries can also help cleanse input before use in your application.

By using parameterized queries, prepared statements, and proper data encoding and validation, developers can shield their applications from these prevalent threats. Implementing Content Security Policies further hardens applications against XSS, ensuring that the application behaves as intended without unexpected script executions.

OAuth2 and JWT for Secure Data Access

OAuth2 is an authorization framework that enables applications to obtain limited access to user accounts on an HTTP service, such as Facebook, GitHub, or Google. It works by delegating user authentication to the service that hosts the user account and authorizing third-party applications to access the user. JSON Web Tokens (JWT) are an open, industry standard RFC 7519 method for representing claims securely between two parties.

Implementing OAuth2

To integrate OAuth2 in a Go application, you can use the **golang.org/x/oauth2** package, which provides support for making OAuth2 authorized and authenticated HTTP requests.

- **Choose an OAuth2 Provider**: First, you need to create a project in the Google Developer Console and set up the OAuth consent screen.
- **Create Credentials**: In the Google Developer Console, create credentials to get the client ID and client secret needed for the OAuth flow.
- **Install OAuth2 Package**: Install the Go OAuth2 package.

```
go get golang.org/x/oauth2
```

- **Implement OAuth2**: Following is how to set up the OAuth2 configuration and handle the redirection for authentication.

```
package main


import (
 "golang.org/x/oauth2"
 "golang.org/x/oauth2/google"
 "net/http"
)


var (
 googleOauthConfig = &oauth2.Config{
 RedirectURL: "http://localhost:8080/callback",
```

```
ClientID: "your-client-id",

ClientSecret: "your-client-secret",

Scopes:
[]string{"https://www.googleapis.com/auth/userinfo.email"
},

Endpoint: google.Endpoint,

}

// Some random string, random for each request

oauthStateString = "pseudo-random"

)


func handleGoogleLogin(w http.ResponseWriter, r
*http.Request) {

url := googleOauthConfig.AuthCodeURL(oauthStateString)

http.Redirect(w, r, url, http.StatusTemporaryRedirect)

}


func handleGoogleCallback(w http.ResponseWriter, r
*http.Request) {

state := r.FormValue("state")

if state != oauthStateString {

http.Error(w, "state did not match",
http.StatusBadRequest)
```

```
return

}


code := r.FormValue("code")

token, err :=
googleOauthConfig.Exchange(oauth2.NoContext, code)

if err != nil {

http.Error(w, "code exchange failed: "+err.Error(),
http.StatusInternalServerError)

return

}


response, err :=
http.Get("https://www.googleapis.com/oauth2/v2/userinfo?a
ccess_token=" + token.AccessToken)

if err != nil {

http.Error(w, "failed getting user info: "+err.Error(),
http.StatusInternalServerError)

return

}

defer response.Body.Close()


// Process the user info and possibly store it in your
database
```

```
}
```

This above code configures OAuth2 with Google and handles the login and callback routes where Google redirects the user after authentication.

Implementing JWT for Secure Data Access

JWT is used to securely transmit information between parties as a JSON object. This information can be verified and trusted because it is digitally signed.

- Install the JWT Package:

```
go get -u github.com/dgrijalva/jwt-go
```

- Create and Validate Tokens:

```
package main


import (
 "github.com/dgrijalva/jwt-go"
 "time"
 "net/http"
)


var mySigningKey = []byte("secret")


func createToken(w http.ResponseWriter, r *http.Request)
{
 token := jwt.New(jwt.SigningMethodHS256)
 claims := token.Claims.(jwt.MapClaims)
```

```
claims["authorized"] = true
claims["user"] = "John Doe"
claims["exp"] = time.Now().Add(time.Hour * 1).Unix()

tokenString, error := token.SignedString(mySigningKey)
if error != nil {
http.Error(w, error.Error(),
http.StatusInternalServerError)
return
}

w.Write([]byte(tokenString))
}

func validateToken(w http.ResponseWriter, r
*http.Request) {
tokenString := r.Header.Get("Authorization")
claims := &jwt.MapClaims{}
token, error := jwt.ParseWithClaims(tokenString, claims,
func(token *jwt.Token) (interface{}, error) {
return mySigningKey, nil
```

```
})

if error != nil {
http.Error(w, error.Error(),
http.StatusInternalServerError)
return
}

if token.Valid {
w.Write([]byte(fmt.Sprintf("Hello, %s",
(*claims)["user"])))
} else {
http.Error(w, "Invalid token", http.StatusUnauthorized)
}
}
```

This setup creates a JWT when the user logs in and validates it on subsequent requests. The token includes claims that you can check to grant access to protected resources.

Summary

In this chapter, we covered the basics of Go application security, including how to use strong protocols to protect web interactions and what security practices are essential. Beginning with secure coding practices, the chapter covered a range of topics including binary and source code checks, dependency updates, and the use of tools like Go's vet command and race detection. Next, we went over how to set up TLS/SSL protocols to secure data transmission between clients and servers, followed by learning how to integrate HTTPS using Go's crypto/tls package. All communications are encrypted with this setup, guaranteeing their secrecy and authenticity. The next step was to deal with the security of HTTP headers and cookies. To prevent common web vulnerabilities like cross-site request forgery and cross-site scripting, strategies were shown to be effective in configuring cookies with flags like SameSite, HttpOnly, and secure.

The chapter continued by teaching ways to protect against SQL injections and cross-site scripting attacks, with examples to back up the claims. Secure data access using OAuth2 and JWT was also covered in the chapter. Using JWT for session management and API security, and OAuth2 for user authentication with third-party providers, the process was mastered step by step. In sum, this chapter served as a thorough reference for bolstering the safety of Go apps via careful coding, encrypted communication, and stringent data validation procedures.

CHAPTER 9: TESTING AND DEBUGGING GO APPLICATIONS

Chapter Overview

In this chapter, we will go through testing and debugging Go applications. This chapter explains in depth how to use techniques like systematic testing, profiling, logging, and debugging to improve the quality of Go code.

As a first step, we will look at Unit Testing with Testify, an add-on for Go's testing package that streamlines the testing process with features like assertions and mocking to make your tests easier to read and maintain. The goal of this chapter is to teach you how to use Testify to create thorough unit tests for your application components. After we finish with unit testing, we will look into using GoMock to mock dependencies. With this tool, you can model the effects of complicated dependencies on your tests. To test components independently of their external dependencies, developers can use GoMock to build mock implementations of interfaces. This allows them to test one piece at a time.

Next, the chapter explores pprof, a tool that developers can use to analyze and optimize their Go apps, by going into Profiling Go Apps. This section will teach you how to use pprof to record and assess application performance metrics like memory allocation and CPU utilization with the help of real-world examples. The next topic is Run Logging with Zerolog, a logging library made for structured and leveled logging that is very fast. With zerolog, you get a simple logger that is quick and can process large amounts of logs with little impact on performance.

Lastly, the chapter finishes with Delve, a debugger made specifically for Go, and how to use it for debugging and troubleshooting. At any given moment, developers can halt the execution of their program, inspect its state, and see its behavior with Delve. You will learn how to set up Delve, create breakpoints, and inspect variables in this section so that you can troubleshoot and fix software problems.

You are going to finish this chapter with a firm grasp of the techniques and resources needed to test, profile, and debug Go applications efficiently and effectively, laying the groundwork for the development of high-quality, error-free software.

Unit Testing with Testify

Software development would be incomplete without unit testing, which entails checking the functionality of specific parts of an application to make sure they function as intended. In Go, while the standard library provides basic testing tools, Testify is a popular third-party library that extends Go's **`testing`** package, offering more powerful features for assertions and mocking, which simplify writing comprehensive and readable tests.

What is Testify?

Testify is a toolkit with several packages that make it easier to write unit tests. It includes:

- The **`assert`** package for more expressive assertions,
- The **`require`** package that stops test execution when a test fails,
- The **`suite`** package for organizing tests into suites, and
- The **`mock`** package for mocking interfaces.

These tools help developers write more structured and easier-to-manage tests.

Installing Testify

To begin using Testify, you first need to install the package in your Go project and then add Testify by running:

```
go get github.com/stretchr/testify
```

This command downloads Testify and its dependencies, making them available in your project.

Writing First Test with Testify

To demonstrate how to use Testify for unit testing, we consider a simple Go application that includes a service for managing books in a library. We will write tests for this service using Testify.

Define Book Service

First, we define a simple service in your Go application that allows adding books and retrieving them.

```
package library


type Book struct {
 Title string
 Author string
 ISBN string
}
```

```go
type BookService struct {
 books []Book
}

func NewBookService() *BookService {
 return &BookService{}
}

func (s *BookService) AddBook(b Book) {
 s.books = append(s.books, b)
}

func (s *BookService) GetAllBooks() []Book {
 return s.books
}
```

Setup Test Files and Write Tests

Create a new file called **book_service_test.go** in the same package where your service is defined. In the test file, import the necessary packages, including Testify's **assert** package for making assertions:

```go
package library
```

```
import (
 "testing"
 "github.com/stretchr/testify/assert"
)

func TestAddBook(t *testing.T) {
 service := NewBookService()
 book := Book{Title: "1984", Author: "George Orwell",
ISBN: "1234567890"}

 service.AddBook(book)
 assert.Equal(t, 1, len(service.GetAllBooks()), "Book was
not added")
 assert.Equal(t, "1984", service.GetAllBooks()[0].Title,
"Book title does not match")
}

func TestGetAllBooks(t *testing.T) {
 service := NewBookService()
 book1 := Book{Title: "1984", Author: "George Orwell",
ISBN: "1234567890"}
 book2 := Book{Title: "Brave New World", Author: "Aldous
Huxley", ISBN: "0987654321"}
```

```
service.AddBook(book1)
service.AddBook(book2)


allBooks := service.GetAllBooks()
assert.Equal(t, 2, len(allBooks), "Incorrect number of
books returned")
assert.Equal(t, "Brave New World", allBooks[1].Title,
"Book title does not match")
}
```

These tests use Testify's **assert** functions to check conditions within the tests. The **assert.Equal** function checks if the expected and actual values are equal, and it will report an error in a user-friendly manner if they are not.

Running Tests

To run your tests, use the **go test** command in your terminal:

```
go test ./...
```

This command will execute all tests in your project, and Testify will help format any errors found during testing, making it easier to identify and fix issues.

Mocking Dependencies with GoMock

In software testing, particularly unit testing, mocking dependencies involves creating mock versions of complex objects or systems that a component under test interacts with. It isolates the component being tested from the behavior of its external dependencies, ensuring that tests are focused, deterministic, and fast. By mocking dependencies, you can simulate various scenarios and behaviors that might not be easy or practical to reproduce with real objects, such as error conditions, rare events, or lengthy operations.

What is GoMock?

GoMock is a popular mocking framework for the Go programming language. It integrates seamlessly with Go's built-in testing framework, allowing developers to generate and use mock objects within their tests. GoMock is particularly powerful due to its ability to generate mocks from interfaces, making it possible to mimic any component that fulfills an interface.

Installing GoMock

To use GoMock in your Go projects, you first need to install it. You can do this using **go get**:

```
go get github.com/golang/mock/mockgen
```

This command installs the **mockgen** tool, which is used to generate source files that contain mocked implementations based on given interfaces.

Setting up GoMock for Project

After installing GoMock, the next step is to set it up within your project as below:

```
package store


type Database interface {
 GetUser(id string) (User, error)
 AddUser(user User) error
}
```

You would use **mockgen** to generate a mock implementation of this **Database** interface:

```
mockgen -source=store/database.go -
destination=store/mock_store/mock_database.go -
package=mock_store
```

The above command tells **mockgen** to read the **store/database.go** file, generate mocks for interfaces found there, and write the output to **store/mock_store/mock_database.go** under the package **mock_store**.

Writing Tests using GoMock

Now that you have a mocked version of your **Database** interface, you can use it to write unit tests for components that depend on this interface. Suppose you have a service that uses the **Database** to manage users:

```
package service

import "github.com/myapp/store"

type UserService struct {
 db store.Database
}

func (s *UserService) CreateUser(user store.User) error {
 return s.db.AddUser(user)
}
```

Given below is how you might write a test for **UserService.CreateUser** using the mocked **Database**:

```
package service

import (
 "testing"
 "github.com/golang/mock/gomock"
 "github.com/myapp/store"
```

```go
"github.com/myapp/store/mock_store"
)

func TestCreateUser(t *testing.T) {
ctrl := gomock.NewController(t)
defer ctrl.Finish()

mockDB := mock_store.NewMockDatabase(ctrl)
user := store.User{ID: "1", Name: "John Doe"}

mockDB.EXPECT().AddUser(gomock.Eq(user)).Return(nil)

userService := UserService{db: mockDB}
err := userService.CreateUser(user)
if err != nil {
t.Errorf("Expected no error, got %v", err)
}
}
```

In this test,

- A **`gomock.Controller`** is created to manage the lifecycle of the mock objects.
- A **`MockDatabase`** is created and configured to expect a call to **`AddUser`** with a specific user and to return **`nil`**, indicating success.

- The **UserService** is then tested to ensure it behaves as expected when **AddUser** succeeds.

With GoMock, you can surely simulate any behavior of dependencies needed for thorough testing, including failures, edge cases, and non-standard responses, all without having to rely on those external systems being available or behaving consistently.

Profiling Go Apps using 'pprof'

When you profile an application, you look at how it runs in different metrics, like how much memory and CPU it uses and how often and for how long it calls functions. If you want to find performance issues, learn how an app acts in different scenarios, and optimize it, this is the process for you. Profiling helps developers understand how to make their code better and more efficient.

What is pprof?

pprof is a tool for visualization and analysis of profiling data. It is part of the Go toolchain and collects profiling data from a live program or from a saved profile generated by the program. **pprof** can analyze CPU, heap, goroutine, thread creation, and block (contention) profiles.

Setting up Profiling

To profile a Go application using **pprof**, you need to import the **net/http/pprof** package and then expose it via an HTTP server. This allows **pprof** to hook into your application and collect profiling data while it's running.

Integrate pprof with Go Application

Given below is how to add **pprof** to a simple web server:

```
package main


import (
 "log"
 "net/http"
 _ "net/http/pprof"
)
```

```
func main() {
 http.HandleFunc("/", func(w http.ResponseWriter, r
*http.Request) {
 w.Write([]byte("Hello, world!"))
 })

 log.Println("Starting server on :8080")
 log.Fatal(http.ListenAndServe(":8080", nil))
}
```

By importing **net/http/pprof**, you automatically add several routes to the default HTTP muxer which the **http.ListenAndServe** uses. These routes are used to access profiling data.

Running Your Application

Start your application as you normally would. If it's already running, ensure it includes the **pprof** routes.

Accessing Profiling Data

Once your application is running with **pprof** enabled, you can access profiling data through various following **pprof** endpoints:

- **Heap Profile**: Visit **http://localhost:8080/debug/pprof/heap** to get a snapshot of the memory allocation of your application.
- **CPU Profile**: Start a CPU profile by accessing **http://localhost:8080/debug/pprof/profile?seconds=30**. This endpoint collects 30 seconds of CPU profiling data (you can adjust the duration).
- **Goroutine Profile**: Check currently running goroutines by visiting **http://localhost:8080/debug/pprof/goroutine**.
- **Full Profile List**: Visit **http://localhost:8080/debug/pprof/** to see all

available profiles.

Analyzing Profile Data

To analyze the collected data, you can download the profile and use the **`go tool pprof`** command. For example, to analyze a CPU profile:

```
wget http://localhost:8080/debug/pprof/profile?seconds=30

go tool pprof profile
```

Once you are in the **`pprof`** tool, you can use various commands to analyze the profile data:

- **`top`**: Shows the top functions where CPU time is spent.
- **`list [function name]`**: Shows the annotated source of the function.
- **`web`**: Generates a graph in SVG format showing call graph.

Consider you have a Go server that processes some data in a computationally intensive way. By running the server with **`pprof`** enabled, and then accessing the CPU profile, you could determine which functions are causing the most load and optimize them. Profiling with **`pprof`** allows you to measure where resources are being used most intensively and identify parts of your code that may cause performance issues.

Run Logging with Zerolog

Zerolog is a high-performance, zero-allocation JSON logger that offers structured logging with a simple and clean API that enables you to produce and consume logs that are easy to read and parse by both humans and machines. This alone makes Zerolog particularly well-suited for modern, large-scale applications that rely on automated log processing and analysis.

Installing Zerolog

To integrate Zerolog into your Go project, you first need to add it as a dependency:

```
go get -u github.com/rs/zerolog/log
```

This command retrieves the Zerolog package and makes it available in your project.

Setting up Zerolog

To start using Zerolog in your project, you need to import it and configure a basic logger setup. Zerolog can be configured to log in different formats, including console-friendly human-readable format and JSON format, which is more suitable for production environments where logs might be consumed by log management tools.

Following is a basic setup for both development and production environments:

```
package main


import (
 "os"
 "time"


 "github.com/rs/zerolog"
 "github.com/rs/zerolog/log"
)


func setupLogger() {
 // Log as JSON instead of the default ASCII formatter.
 log.Logger = log.Output(zerolog.ConsoleWriter{Out:
os.Stderr, TimeFormat: time.RFC3339})


 // Set global log level
 zerolog.SetGlobalLevel(zerolog.InfoLevel)


 // In production, you might want to change to
zerolog.InfoLevel and log to a file:
```

```
// file, _ := os.Create("log.txt")
// log.Logger = log.Output(zerolog.ConsoleWriter{Out:
file, TimeFormat: time.RFC3339})
}

func main() {
 setupLogger()

 log.Info().Msg("This is an informational message")
 log.Error().Msg("This is an error message")

 simulateProcess()
}

func simulateProcess() {
 for i := 0; i < 5; i++ {
 log.Debug().Int("iteration", i).Msg("Simulating
process")
 time.Sleep(1 * time.Second)
 }

 log.Warn().Msg("Simulation completed with a warning")
```

```
}
```

In the above sample program, the **setupLogger** function configures the global logger to output messages to the console in a human-readable format with timestamps. In a production environment, you might prefer logging in JSON format to a file, which can be adjusted easily with Zerolog.

Sample Program: Logging using Zerolog

Let us consider that we integrated Zerolog into GitforGits, which could be to manage various operations such as user management, repository handling, etc. Given below is how you might add detailed logging to a function that handles file uploads to a repository:

```
func uploadFileToRepo(filename string, data []byte) error
{

 log.Debug().

 Str("filename", filename).

 Int("size", len(data)).

 Msg("Uploading file to repository")


 if err := ioutil.WriteFile(filename, data, 0644); err !=
nil {

 log.Error().

 Str("filename", filename).

 Err(err).

 Msg("Failed to upload file")

 return err

 }
```

```
log.Info().
Str("filename", filename).
Msg("File uploaded successfully")
return nil
}
```

In this function, Zerolog is used to log debug information about the file being uploaded, report errors if the upload fails, and confirm success when the upload completes. This level of logging is invaluable for debugging and monitoring the behavior of your application, especially in production environments.

Debugging and Troubleshooting with Delve

If you are looking for a Go debugger, Delve is a great choice because it's more powerful and easier to use than GDB (GNU Debugger). For starting, stopping, inspecting, and modifying Go programs, it offers a thorough and user-friendly interface.

Installing Delve

You can install Delve using **go get**:

```
go install github.com/go-delve/delve/cmd/dlv@latest
```

This above command fetches and installs the Delve debugger into your Go bin directory, making it accessible from anywhere on your system. When it comes to using it, Delve can be easily used through its command-line interface or via integration with various IDEs like Visual Studio Code, GoLand, or Atom. To begin debugging with Delve from the command line, navigate to your project directory and start a debugging session:

```
dlv debug
```

This command compiles your program with optimizations disabled (to improve debugging experience), launches it, and attaches a debugger to it.

Sample Program: Debugging Scenarios

We will explore how to use Delve to debug various scenarios in a Go project. We will consider a simple Go application that has a few functions, demonstrating typical debugging tasks.

Scenario 1: Investigating Panic

Suppose you have a Go function that occasionally panics due to an index out of range error, and you need to determine what's going wrong.

```
package main

import "fmt"

func buggyFunction(data []int) {
 fmt.Println("Accessing out of range element:", data[10])
// Intentional bug
}

func main() {
 data := []int{1, 2, 3}
 buggyFunction(data)
}
```

To debug this, run Delve, set a breakpoint at the function, and inspect variables:

```
$ dlv debug
(dlv) break main.buggyFunction
(dlv) continue
(dlv) print data
```

Delve will stop execution at the breakpoint, allowing you to inspect the **data** slice and realize that it doesn't have enough elements, leading to panic.

Scenario 2: Stepping through Code

Next, let us say you want to step through the code to understand the flow of a more complex function:

```
func complexFunction(numbers []int) int {
 sum := 0
 for _, num := range numbers {
 sum += num
 }
 return sum
}

func main() {
 numbers := []int{1, 2, 3, 4, 5}
 result := complexFunction(numbers)
 fmt.Println("Sum:", result)
}
```

To step through **complexFunction**:

```
(dlv) break main.complexFunction
(dlv) continue
(dlv) next
(dlv) print sum
```

```
(dlv) next
```

Using **next** allows you to move one line at a time within the same function, observing how the state of your program changes.

Scenario 3: Altering Execution

Consider you are debugging and realize you want to test how the function behaves with different data without stopping your session:

```
func displayMessage(count int) {

 if count > 5 {

 fmt.Println("Count is high")

 } else {

 fmt.Println("Count is low")

 }

}


func main() {

 displayMessage(3)

}
```

Debug and change the variable:

```
(dlv) break main.displayMessage

(dlv) continue

(dlv) set count = 10

(dlv) continue
```

The above command sequence sets a new value for **`count`** and continues execution, allowing you to see how changes affect your program's flow and output without restarting the debugger. Debugging with Delve helps uncover subtle bugs and understand complex application behaviors, making it an invaluable tool for any Go developer looking to improve the robustness and reliability of their applications.

Summary

Overall, this chapter provided you with the knowledge needed to effectively enhance software quality by focusing on the essential tools and techniques for testing and debugging Go applications. First, we learned how to use the Testify toolkit, which enhances Go's native testing capabilities, for unit testing. After getting a handle on unit testing, the focus moved to GoMock dependency mocking. The ability to test units independently was made possible by this robust library, which facilitated the simulation of complex systems. It is another robust library for interactions within tests.

You then had the opportunity to integrate pprof, a powerful tool for profiling Go applications, to collect and analyze performance metrics. This helped you to identify performance bottlenecks and optimize code efficiency. The chapter continued by introducing Zerolog, a framework for efficient and organized logging that can be used to track application behavior and identify problems in staging and live environments.

Last but not least, the chapter wrapped up with debugging techniques for inspecting and manipulating program execution using the Delve debugger. This tool was vital to effectively troubleshooting complicated issues and conducting in-depth analyses of code behavior.

Chapter 10: Deploying Go Applications

Chapter Overview

This chapter explores the practical aspects of deploying Go applications, with a particular emphasis on the techniques and strategies that guarantee scalable, maintainable, and robust deployments. If you are a developer interested in learning about the entire development to production cycle of a Go application, you must read this chapter.

First, you'll get a practical understanding of Dockerfiles, Docker images, and the process of running Go applications inside Docker containers as you learn about containerization in this chapter. The chapter then moves on to teach deployment strategies, such as blue-green and canary deployments.

The specifics of deploying Go apps on AWS are covered in the 'Deploying to AWS' section. In this section, you will learn how to host, manage, and scale Go applications using AWS services such as EC2, ECS, and RDS. Also included is some helpful advice on how to use AWS's elastic capabilities to deal with fluctuating loads. The next part, 'Environment and Configuration Management', introduces Viper as a tool for efficiently managing application settings and configurations in all stages of an application's lifecycle, from development to testing to production.

You will leave this chapter with a solid practical grasp of managing and deploying Go applications in a production environment, making sure you are ready to handle real-world application deployment scenarios with ease.

Containerization with Docker

Containerization is a lightweight form of virtualization that allows you to run and manage applications along with their dependencies in a process-isolated environment called a container. Unlike traditional virtualization, which requires entire virtual operating systems, containerization involves encapsulating an application in a container with its own runtime environment, thereby using the host system's kernel. This approach provides significant benefits in terms of resource efficiency, scalability, and portability.

Why Docker for Containerization?

Docker is one of the most popular containerization platforms. It enables the packaging of an application and its dependencies into a container that can be executed consistently on any Docker engine, regardless of the underlying infrastructure. This consistency addresses the common "it works on my machine" problem, as Docker ensures that it works everywhere.

Dockerizing Go Application

To demonstrate the process of containerizing a Go application, we consider a simple web server written in Go. This server will serve a basic HTTP response. We will then dockerize this application.

Create a Go Web Server

First, create a Go file named **main.go**. This file will include a simple HTTP server:

```
package main


import (
 "fmt"
 "net/http"
)


func main() {
 http.HandleFunc("/", func(w http.ResponseWriter, r
*http.Request) {
 fmt.Fprintln(w, "Hello, Docker!")
 })


 fmt.Println("Server is running on port 8080")
 http.ListenAndServe(":8080", nil)
}
```

This program sets up a web server that listens on port 8080 and responds with "Hello, Docker!" when accessed.

Write Dockerfile

A Dockerfile is a text document that contains all the commands needed to build a Docker image. Create a file named **Dockerfile** in the same directory as your Go file:

```
# Use the official Golang image to create a build
artifact.

# This is based on Debian and sets the GOPATH to /go.

FROM golang:1.16 as builder


# Create and change to the app directory.

WORKDIR /app


# Retrieve application dependencies.

# This allows the container build to reuse cached
dependencies.

COPY go.mod go.sum ./

RUN go mod download


# Copy local code to the container image.

COPY . ./


# Build the binary.

# -o myapp specifies the output file name, reducing
ambiguity.

RUN CGO_ENABLED=0 GOOS=linux go build -v -o myapp
```

```
# Use a Docker multi-stage build to create a lean production image.

# https://docs.docker.com/develop/develop-images/multistage-build/

# Start from a Debian image with the latest version of Go installed

# and a workspace (GOPATH) configured at /go.

FROM golang:1.16


# Copy the binary to the production image from the builder stage.

COPY --from=builder /app/myapp /myapp


# Run the web service on container startup.

CMD ["/myapp"]
```

Build Docker Image

Run the following command in your terminal in the directory containing your Dockerfile:

```
docker build -t go-docker-app .
```

This command builds the Docker image with the tag **go-docker-app** using the Dockerfile in the current directory.

Run Docker Container

After building the image, run your container:

```
docker run -p 8080:8080 go-docker-app
```

The above command runs your Docker container and maps port 8080 of the container to port 8080 on your host, allowing you to access the Go web server via **localhost:8080** in your browser.

By streamlining deployments and guaranteeing consistency across environments, this entire process improves the application's scalability and reliability, decreases development and support costs, and more. Higher utilization densities in production environments are possible with Docker because it uses system resources more efficiently than traditional virtual machines.

Deployment Strategies

In modern application deployment, having a robust deployment strategy is crucial to minimize downtime and ensure a seamless user experience. We will explore and demonstrate three popular deployment strategies: rolling, canary, and blue-green deployments. Each has its benefits and is suited to different scenarios depending on the needs for reliability, speed, and risk mitigation.

Rolling Deployment

A rolling deployment gradually replaces instances of the previous version of an application with instances of the new version without downtime. It is typically automated and managed by orchestrators like Kubernetes.

Suppose you have a basic Go web application containerized with Docker, and you want to deploy a new version using a rolling update in a Kubernetes environment.

- First, ensure you have a Kubernetes cluster running. You can use Minikube for a local setup.
- Create a deployment and expose it:

```
# deployment.yaml
apiVersion: apps/v1
kind: Deployment
metadata:
  name: go-app-deployment
spec:
```

```
replicas: 3
selector:
matchLabels:
app: go-app
template:
metadata:
labels:
app: go-app
spec:
containers:
- name: go-app
image: go-app:v1
ports:
- containerPort: 8080
---
apiVersion: v1
kind: Service
metadata:
 name: go-app-service
spec:
 selector:
```

```
app: go-app
ports:
- protocol: TCP
port: 80
targetPort: 8080
type: LoadBalancer
```

- Deploy this using **kubectl apply -f deployment.yaml**.
- To update to **go-app:v2**, you can run:

```
kubectl set image deployment/go-app-deployment go-app=go-app:v2 --record
```

Kubernetes will begin replacing the old pods with new pods one by one, ensuring there's no downtime.

Canary Deployment

Canary deployment involves rolling out the new version to a small subset of users before making it available to everybody. This strategy is useful for testing the new version in the live environment with a small portion of the traffic.

Consider that we want to modify the existing Kubernetes configuration to direct a portion of the traffic to the new version.

In this, you will have two deployments: one for the stable version and one for the canary version.

```
# For the canary deployment
apiVersion: apps/v1
kind: Deployment
metadata:
  name: go-app-canary
```

```
spec:
 replicas: 1 # fewer replicas for canary
 selector:
 matchLabels:
 app: go-app
 track: canary
 template:
 metadata:
 labels:
 app: go-app
 track: canary
 spec:
 containers:
 - name: go-app
 image: go-app:v2
 ports:
 - containerPort: 8080
```

Deploy the canary by applying this configuration. Then, adjust the service to load-balance traffic between the stable and canary versions:

```
spec:
 selector:
 app: go-app
```

```
ports:
- protocol: TCP
port: 80
targetPort: 8080
type: LoadBalancer
```

Blue-Green Deployment

Blue-green deployment is a strategy where two identical environments are maintained. The new version is deployed to the green environment while the blue one serves live traffic. Once the new version is tested and ready, the traffic is switched from blue to green.

Now, for a blue-green deployment, you need two environments. Assuming the blue environment is currently active, you deploy the green environment:

```
# Green deployment configuration
apiVersion: apps/v1
kind: Deployment
metadata:
 name: go-app-green
spec:
 replicas: 3
 selector:
 matchLabels:
 app: go-app
 stage: green
 template:
```

```
metadata:
labels:
app: go-app
stage: green
spec:
containers:
- name: go-app
image: go-app:v2
ports:
- containerPort: 8080
```

Deploy this configuration. To switch traffic to the green environment, update the service selector:

```
# Update to the service configuration
spec:
 selector:
 app: go-app
 stage: green # Change this from blue to green
```

Depending on your operational needs and risk tolerance, each of the deployment strategies mentioned above offers distinct advantages. You can test in production with limited scope with canary releases, have maximum control with blue-green deployments, and avoid downtime with rolling updates.

Deploying to AWS CodeDeploy

Now that the GitforGits project has been successfully containerized using Docker and all the necessary configurations, like the Go web server and Dockerfile, have been setup, the next step is to configure AWS CodeDeploy to deploy the Dockerized application onto AWS services. To avoid duplicating efforts, we will concentrate on setting up AWS CodeDeploy and starting the deployment process.

Upload Docker Image to Amazon ECR

Since the Docker image is already prepared, you need to push it to Amazon Elastic Container Registry (ECR), which will be used by AWS CodeDeploy for deployment.

- Create an ECR Repository:
  - Navigate to the Amazon ECR console.
  - Click "Create repository".
  - Name your repository (e.g., **gitforgits**).
- Authenticate Docker to Your ECR Repository:

```
aws ecr get-login-password --region your-region | docker
login --username AWS --password-stdin your-account-
id.dkr.ecr.your-region.amazonaws.com
```

- Tag Your Docker Image:

```
docker tag gitforgits:latest your-account-
id.dkr.ecr.your-region.amazonaws.com/gitforgits:latest
```

- Push the Image to ECR:

```
docker push your-account-id.dkr.ecr.your-
region.amazonaws.com/gitforgits:latest
```

Create CodeDeploy Application and Deployment Group

Assuming the IAM roles and EC2 instance roles are already configured:

- Create a CodeDeploy Application:
  - Open the AWS CodeDeploy console.
  - Click on "Create application".
  - Name your application (e.g., **GitforGitsApp**), select "EC2/On-premises" for the compute platform.

- Create a Deployment Group:
  - Assign it a name (e.g., **GitforGitsDeploymentGroup**).
  - Choose the previously created **CodeDeployRole**.
  - Select in-place deployment type.
  - Set up a load balancer if your application is production-critical (optional).

Configure appspec.yml file for Deployment

The **appspec.yml** file is crucial for defining the deployment actions and hooking lifecycle events.

```
version: 0.0
os: linux
files:
 - source: /
 destination: /var/gitforgits
hooks:
 ApplicationStop:
 - location: scripts/stop_application.sh
 timeout: 30
 BeforeInstall:
 - location: scripts/cleanup_before_install.sh
 timeout: 30
 AfterInstall:
 - location: scripts/change_permissions.sh
 timeout: 30
```

```
ApplicationStart:
- location: scripts/start_application.sh
timeout: 30
ValidateService:
- location: scripts/validate_service.sh
timeout: 30
```

Make sure all script paths in the **appspec.yml** reflect actual scripts that handle each deployment lifecycle event appropriately.

Deploy using AWS CodeDeploy

- Bundle your **appspec.yml** and necessary scripts into a zip file and upload it to an S3 bucket.
- In the CodeDeploy application dashboard:
  - Select your application and deployment group.
  - Choose the revision by specifying the S3 bucket and zip file.
  - Deploy the revision.

Monitor and Verify Deployment

- Use the AWS CodeDeploy dashboard to monitor the deployment process. Check the deployment details for logs and status updates.
- Ensure the application is running as expected. This might involve checking logs, making test HTTP requests, or using monitoring tools to verify performance and functionality.

For a dependable and scalable deployment process that keeps the application up and running, use AWS CodeDeploy. This takes advantage of AWS's robust environment. In addition to improving the overall deployment workflow, this simplified method streamlines deployment tasks, making it easier to accommodate updates and scaling needs.

Environment and Configuration Management using Viper

Introduction to Viper

Viper is a popular configuration management library designed for Go applications. It supports handling configuration from a variety of sources including JSON, TOML, YAML, environment variables, and command-line flags. Viper is particularly well-suited for 12-factor applications that require configuration to be stored in external sources to facilitate easy changes without the need for recompilation.

Following are the key attributes of Viper:

- Viper can read configurations from files, environment variables, remote config systems, and the command line.
- Viper can watch config files for changes and re-read them into your application without restarting the app.
- Viper can unmarshal configurations into native Go structures, simplifying the use of complex configurations in the code.

Setting up Viper

To demonstrate the use of Viper in managing configurations, we configure a simple Go application that reads settings from a file and environment variables.

Install Viper

First, add Viper to your Go project:

```
go get github.com/spf13/viper
```

Create Configuration Files

Create a **config.yaml** file in your project directory:

```
port: 8080

hostname: "localhost"

features:

 feature1: true

 feature2: false
```

Configure Viper to Read Config file

Set up Viper in your Go application to read this configuration file. Create a **main.go** file:

```
package main


import (
 "fmt"
 "log"


 "github.com/spf13/viper"
)


func main() {
 viper.SetConfigName("config") // name of config file
(without extension)
 viper.SetConfigType("yaml") // REQUIRED if the config
file does not have the extension in the name
 viper.AddConfigPath(".") // optionally look for config
in the working directory
 err := viper.ReadInConfig() // Find and read the config
file
 if err != nil { // Handle errors reading the config file
 log.Fatalf("Fatal error config file: %s \n", err)
 }
```

```
 fmt.Println("Port:", viper.GetInt("port"))

 fmt.Println("Hostname:", viper.GetString("hostname"))

 fmt.Println("Feature1 Enabled:",
viper.GetBool("features.feature1"))


 // Demonstrating environment variable override

 viper.BindEnv("hostname") // Typically done at
initialization

 viper.SetEnvPrefix("gfg") // will be uppercased
automatically

 fmt.Println("Hostname from ENV:",
viper.GetString("hostname"))

}
```

In this setup, Viper loads configurations from **config.yaml**. It prints out some configurations directly accessed via Viper's getter methods.

Override Configuration with Environment Variables

Viper allows you to override configuration settings using environment variables. For example, if you set an environment variable before running the application:

```
export GFG_HOSTNAME=production-server

go run main.go
```

This change dynamically overrides the **hostname** defined in the **config.yaml** file due to the **BindEnv** call linked to the **hostname** key in Viper's setup. When you run the application, it should reflect this overridden value.

Watch Config File for Changes

Viper can be configured to watch a config file for changes without restarting the application. Given below is how you can implement this feature:

```
viper.WatchConfig()

viper.OnConfigChange(func(e fsnotify.Event) {

 fmt.Println("Config file changed:", e.Name)

 fmt.Println("New Port:", viper.GetInt("port"))

})
```

With this setup, your Go application reacts to changes made in the **config.yaml** file in real time, useful for applications that need to adapt quickly to configuration changes without downtime.

Viper is a powerful tool for managing application configurations in Go projects and its capability is particularly valuable in cloud-native and distributed architectures where external configuration management and dynamic reconfiguration are often required.

Summary

With an emphasis on advanced practices and tools necessary for effective deployment and management in production environments, this chapter offered a thorough attempt at deploying Go applications. The chapter started with Docker containerization, where the idea was defined and the practical steps to package the GitforGits app into Docker containers were shown.

Next, we went over deployment strategies, delving into the minute details of blue-green, canary, and rolling deployments. We explained each tactic in terms of how it benefits in reducing the risks that come with releasing updated software. To guarantee incremental updates and minimize downtime during deployments, these strategies were demonstrated with practical examples.

The next topic was AWS deployment, specifically how to use AWS CodeDeploy to reliably and automatically deploy applications. We demonstrated how to set up AWS CodeDeploy, how to integrate it with other AWS services, and how to deploy it so that you can better manage and deploy your applications.

Environment and configuration management with Viper was also covered in the chapter. The importance of dynamic and cross-environment configuration management for applications was highlighted in this section of the chapter.

In sum, this chapter provided you with the thorough understanding and practical resources necessary to successfully launch, oversee, and protect Go applications in a live setting, guaranteeing that you will be adequately prepared to face the challenges that come with deploying applications in the real world.

Index

Epilogue

In this final section of "Programming Backend with Go," I'd like to take a moment to reflect on everything we've covered so far. This has been a great pleasure to teach you the ins and outs of Go backend development. This book's stated goal was to teach you the fundamentals of Go and how to use them to construct secure, scalable, and reliable backend systems. Along the way, we've learned a lot of different things, but they're all crucial for becoming an expert in backend development.

To maximize Go's potential, we started by establishing a productive development environment, including all of the necessary tools and configurations. A well-prepared environment can greatly simplify your development process, so this essential step is extremely important. After that, we dug into the net/http package, which allows us to build and control web servers. We were able to handle more complex URL patterns and middleware after switching to advanced routing with gorilla/mux, which made our web applications more powerful and flexible.

The utmost importance of safeguarding your applications and user data led to a strong emphasis on security. We discussed typical security flaws, such as SQL injection and cross-site scripting (XSS) attacks, and went over best practices for user authentication with OAuth2 and JWT. You have learnt to create applications that are both useful and resistant to attacks by incorporating these security measures. The efficiency and scalability that Go can offer to SOAs were demonstrated in our investigation of microservices. You have learnt how to build, deploy, and manage microservices using frameworks such as Gin and Kubernetes. This will allow your applications to scale to meet high demand. The use of REST and gRPC for inter-service communication further showcased Go's proficiency in creating efficient and unified systems.

Another significant topic was data management, which GORM facilitated with its robust ORM tool for managing database operations. You have learned all you need to know about data management in applications, from the most fundamental CRUD operations to more complex ones like transaction management and concurrency control. We also looked at how to use NSQ and Apache Kafka for message brokering, which lets you create systems that can manage asynchronous workloads with high throughput. We explored testing and debugging with tools like Testify, GoMock, and Delve, which are essential for maintaining high-quality software. Throughout the book, you learnt the versatile art of coding stability and dependability by creating thorough tests, mocking dependencies, and debugging your applications in an effective manner.

Lastly, we discussed deployment strategies, with an emphasis on blue-green, canary, and rolling deployments. You have learned how to automate your deployment processes with AWS CodeDeploy, guaranteeing that your applications will be delivered smoothly and continuously. I hope that by the time you finish this book, you will be prepared to take on the challenges of backend development in the real world. The goal of creating "Programming Backend with Go" was to make it more than simply a learning resource; it was to make it a reference that you could come back to as your Go programming skills improved. When it comes time to construct, scale, and secure backend systems, the information and expertise you've received will be priceless.

It is my pleasure to have you along for the ride. If you're looking to become a backend developer, I hope this book has given you some great ideas, some useful skills, and some new avenues to explore. Never stop learning, never stop experimenting, and never stop building. I can't wait to see what you come up with next in the expansive and exciting world of Go backend development.

Thank You

Printed in Poland
by Amazon Fulfillment
Poland Sp. z o.o., Wrocław

41170342R00163